THE EDUCATION OF IMMIGRANT CHILDREN

The Education of Immigrant Children

A SOCIAL-PSYCHOLOGICAL INTRODUCTION

A.J. CROPLEY

CROOM HELM
London & Canberra

© 1983 A.J. Cropley
Croom Helm Ltd, Provident House, Burrell Row,
Beckenham, Kent BR3 1AT
Croom Helm Australia, PO Box 391, Manuka,
ACT 2603, Australia

British Library Cataloguing in Publication Data

Cropley, A.J.
    The education of immigrant children.
    1. Children of immigrants——Education——Great Britain
    I. Title
    371.9'7   LC3736.G/

ISBN 0-7099-0788-5

W 23125 /14.95 1183

Typesetting by
Niko Jessen, Hamburg 76, 1983

Printed and bound in Great Britain by
Biddles Ltd, Guildford and King's Lynn

Contents

1. Introduction   11

2. The Immigrant "Problem" in Britain   15

Strangers in our midst   15
What is an immigrant?   17
Who emigrates and why?   19
Historical development of immigration to Britain   21
Focus on West Indians and Pakistanis   25
Differences among people and groups   27
Immigrant children   29
The "problem" of immigrant children   31
Problems of academic achievement   33
Personal problems of immigrant children   36
Closing remarks   37

3. Society, Behaviour and Immigration   39

Societies — A systematic basis for behaviour   39
National self-image   41
The modal personality   43
Societal norms   44
The process of socialization   46
Socialization and group membership   49
Admittance to groups   51
The role of language   54
Implications for studying immigration   57

4. The Homelands: West Indies and Pakistan — 61

Pakistan — 63
  Geographical and historical overview — 65
  Religion — 67
  Social structure — 68
  Family life — 68
  Schooling — 69
  Emigration — 70

West Indies — 71
  Geographical and historical overview — 72
  Social structure — 74
  Family life — 74
  Schooling — 76
  Emigration — 76

Closing remarks — 78

5. Adjusting to a New Society: Process and Problems — 79

Discrepancies in norms — 79
Reaction of the locals — stereotyping — 80
Prejudice — 82
Discrimination — 84
Racism — 87
Assimilation — 88
Assimilation of immigrants in Britain — 92
Alienation in Britain — 94
Rejection of British ways by immigrants — 95
The ghetto phenomenon — 96
Dual alienation — people between two worlds — 99
Dual assimilation — 101
Consequences of alienation — 101
Closing remarks — 104

6. Immigrant Children: Children of Two Worlds   105

Special difficulties of children born in Britain   105
Prejudice among children   108
Children between two worlds   110
Conflict with parents   112
The double bind   114
Alienation from Britain   115
The role of socioeconomic status   118
Self-alienation   121
The role of language   123
Closing remarks   125

7. The Educational Response: Approaches to Date   127

A task for schools   127
The role of school in society   127
Dimensions of the school's response   129
Why have schools been slow to respond?   132
Some possible orientations for change   135
Measures focused on immigrants —
     improved self-image   137
Promoting qualities useful for life in Britain   139
Mastering standard English   141
Some approaches in Britain   143
Experience in the Federal Republic of Germany   147
Measures focused on British children   152
Adapting the entire curriculum   154

8. Conclusions and Suggestions   157

Need for special measures   157
Problems in mastering the English language   159
Resistance to learning English   161
Role of the mother tongue   164

Multicultural schooling   169
- Content of lessons   171
Multicultural perspective   175
Learning materials   176
- Teaching and learning methods   178
Teachers and teacher training   179
The contribution of kindergartens   181
Measures focused on parents   183
Measures focused on the community   184
Research and development   185
Closing thoughts   188

References   191

Index   201

Acknowledgements

Immigration and subsequent adaptation to the receiving society is a subject which lies close to my heart. Having been born and brought up in Australia, I have subsequently spent most of my adult life outside the homeland, especially in Britain, Canada and the Federal Republic of Germany. The experience of being a stranger in a strange land leaves its mark, even on a "transilient" who occupies a privileged position in the receiving society, in my case that of teacher and later professor of psychology. The problems of immigrant parents are also problems which I experience in my own day-to-day life as a result of my interactions with my own sons, citizens of a country they have only visited for short periods of time — long enough to be born there, but little more. I would like to think that these experiences have helped me to reach valuable insights which I can communicate in a convincing manner to both other immigrants and also to non-immigrants.

I had the good fortune to collaborate from 1972 to 1974 with Dr. M. L. Kovacs, Professor of History at the University of Regina in Canada, on the writing of a book concerned with Eastern-European immigrants to Australia. He started me thinking about the psychological aspects of emigration-immigration, and convinced me of the importance of the role of detachment from the norms of the homeland in determining the degree of adaptation to the receiving society. This impetus has now found expression in a series of publications of which this book is one, and I would like to express my indebtedness to him.

1

Introduction

The period of massive inflow of immigrants into Britain is past. Despite this, relations between immigrants and the members of the majority society are, if anything, getting worse. There are already about one million Asian and West Indian "immigrants" in Britain who were actually born here, and the number will go up substantially in the next 20 years. These people can neither be stopped from coming to the United Kingdom nor sent home: they are home already. The real issue in Britain is thus not that of preventing immigrants from arriving, but of developing a society in which the white majority and the black and brown minority can live together in a state of mutual regard and acceptance. The alternative is the development in Britain of a social underclass consisting of alienated immigrants.

The members of the majority white society belong to the group which has been here longest; they thus have a strong and not unjustified feeling that Britain is *their* country. This means that, in some ways, they have the more difficult task in the development of a society in which long-term residents and newcomers can live amicably together. This is because immigrants are already involved in the process of adjusting to change, by virtue of being newcomers. The long-term residents of Britain, on the other hand, are not, and the reasons why they should adapt are far less obvious. Nonetheless, social and personal problems arising out of the presence in Britain of large numbers of immigrants are not exclusively the immigrants' problem, but those of the members of the majority group too. Both groups thus have an interest in achieving a satisfactory adjustment.

The formation of an immigrant underclass, or at the very least of a separate social bloc within the British society, is already under way. The phenomenon is having a wide range of negative consequences. At the everyday level its manifestations include acts of petty spite, such as Whites and Coloureds calling each other contemptuous names. They also include socially "unhealthy" but hard-to-pin-down phenomena such as racial discrimination. Occasionally they manifest themselves in obviously destructive behaviour such as crime, acts of violence or even riots, as recent events have shown. Psychological reactions include, among long-term residents, rejection of immigrants, prejudice and scapegoating. Among immigrants they include the feeling of being fated always to remain an outsider, a sense of disappointment and frustration, or the feeling of being trapped with no future. At the most destructive level the reaction includes anger and rejection of the majority society, or turning against oneself in the form of self-doubt, identity conflict and even mental illness.

Both behavioural and psychological consequences are still mainly confined to the less serious categories previously mentioned. Nonetheless, even these phenomena justify the search for measures aimed at their alleviation. At the governmental level the reaction has been focused on controlling the rate of inflow of immigrants. Where measures have been adopted they have largely been confined to the passing of laws prohibiting incitement to racial hatred, or seeking to eliminate racial discrimination in employment, housing or other public domains. Educational actions have tended to be based on the view that the problem is essentially that of eliminating racial discrimination among the members of the white society. In other words even the limited actions taken to modify relations between groups have mainly involved trying to force people to behave in "virtuous" ways, thus at best attacking the symptoms rather than the disease. In addition, such actions tend to arouse resentment and resistance, even to encourage people to find ways around them, if anything making the underlying attitudes, values, beliefs and motives (the real problem) worse.

The present book, by contrast, concentrates on psychological factors within immigrants, and on the importance of these factors for relations with locals, and for education. It argues, in a nutshell, that immigrants experience a state of estrangement from both their original societies and also from the receiving society. As a result they are "between two worlds". Immigrant children are particularly hard hit, since they have little or no personal acquaintance with the old ways which their parents expect them to espouse, while the British ways with which they may be more familiar often include rejection of the norms of the immigrants' homeland and prejudice against adult immigrants, in this case the youngsters' own parents.

The educational results of this state of affairs manifest themselves partly in poorer achievement on the part of many immigrant children. Lower achievement is in itself a serious enough problem: poor marks prevent the obtaining of qualifications which provide access not only to the job market, but also admission to institutions of higher and further education, with the result that a structural integration of immigrants, in which they occupy positions at the higher as well as the lower levels of the social pecking order, is impossible. However, the clash between norms experienced by many immigrant children also has an effect on their psychological lives, on their sense of self-worth, their feeling of being able and permitted to make a go of things in the local society. Even relatively successful immigrant pupils are not immune to feelings of doubt and diminished worth as human beings, while poor marks and identity problems interact, the one being both a result and also a cause of the other.

Educational reactions to date have largely concentrated on only one aspect of the situation, either seeking to foster high levels of regard for their own origins in immigrants, or else castigating the British for their negative reactions to the strangers in their midst. What is seldom found is a conceptualization of the dual process of simultaneous detachment-attachment which is the heart of adjustment to new societies. Also lacking is a psychological model capable of generating a systematic set of guidelines for the development of desirable educational measures. Such a model is not merely of theoretical interest, but is absolutely essential for the setting of policy and above all for the development of teacher training of an appropriate kind. It would be overly optimistic to propose that the treatment developed in the present book provides the necessary answers. However, it is not unreasonable to hope that it is capable of functioning as a step in the right direction.

The consequences of this state of being between two worlds are discussed with particular regard to West Indian and Pakistani children in Britain, and suggestions made for educational approaches which would reduce the difficulties. The book does not make specific recommendations for concrete classroom actions, nor does it contain curriculum plans or outlines, or review existing curriculum materials such as those developed by the Schools Council. The suggestions made are in the form of guidelines involving shifts of emphasis or altered directions of approach, and are meant to provide an orientation or general approach to the issues at stake, not a package of ready made answers. A major goal of the book is fostering insight and understanding among members of the public, teachers, educational policymakers and teacher educators. It is hoped that this will help in the development of more humane and effective measures for achieving a satisfactory mutual adjustment of immigrants and long-term residents. The book is also intended as a textbook containing a psychological introduction to the area of multiracial education, both for teachers in the initial phase of training and also for practising teachers who wish to develop their understanding of psychological principles in the area.

2
The Immigrant "Problem" in Britain

Strangers in our midst

Several million "strangers" now live in Britain. Of these about 2 million are "coloured", a figure which natural increase will swell to about 3 million by the year 2000, even if there is no further immigration. This means that about 3.5 per cent of the population of the United Kingdom consists of "immigrants" from the "New Commonwealth". Although it is customary to regard coloured residents of this country as foreigners, the fact of the matter is that about one third of them were born here, so that they are not really foreign at all. Despite this the majority of them, easily recognisable from their darker skins and sometimes from their language, dress, food habits, social customs and the like, remain outsiders in many important respects. For example they work at the jobs least desired by the white majority, in occupations which are poorly paid, hard, dirty, boring or otherwise undesirable, and live in the poorer parts of the cities in which they reside. They also experience a certain degree of estrangement from the cultures into which they were born or which, in the case of children and young people, their parents often still espouse. Thus, whether born inside or outside the UK, they are torn between two worlds.

Before proceeding, it is essential that a number of key terms in this and following discussions should be clarified. Several common expressions used in the book, such as "immigrant", have meanings in general usage which are, although clear to members of the public, actually incorrect in a strict sense. For example a person of West Indian origin born here of parents who have been in this country for many years is not really an immigrant at all, but is a UK citizen. Pakistan ceased to be a member of the Commonwealth on September 1st, 1973. Despite these facts, both the West Indian mentioned above and a Pakistani would be referred to by many members of the public as "immigrants" from the "New Commonwealth". Hopefully the use of a number of expressions in the everyday way will not cause offence and will not be taken as indicating lack of concern about the issues involved.

Although "coloured immigrants" constitute less than 4 per cent of the total population of the United Kingdom, about three quarters of them live in Greater London and the West Midlands (Verma and Mallick, 1978), especially in the urban areas of concentration comprised by Birmingham, Leeds, Bradford, Leicester and Wolverhampton. In these regions in particular they play a significant if not crucial role in the transport, engineering, catering, hospital and garment industries, as well as providing a high proportion of the unskilled labour. In parts of London it is possible to pass a dozen pedestrians in the street before encountering a "genuine" British person. There are Local Education Authorities in which more than 50 per cent of all pupils are of immigrant origin, while for about a dozen years there have been schools in which the proportion of immigrant children is as high as 80 per cent (Townsend, 1971). The 1981 census showed not only that the proportion of immigrants in London and the Metropolitan Counties was nearly twice as high as in the rest of Britain, but that there are now five parliamentary constituencies in which more than 40 per cent of the population are in immigrant households. Thus, the strangers now constitute a small but significant part of life in this country, and cannot be ignored.

A second preliminary point needs to be cleared up at this juncture, as readers may notice discrepancies in the statistical data cited here and those in other places in this book or in other sources. There are several reasons for this: data have been taken from a number of different sources, some of them secondary in nature; different sources use different methods of calculating or classifying data; some of the data are only estimates. A specific problem is that after the secession of

Bangladesh in 1971 some people who had previously been classified as Pakistanis ceased to be treated in this way. A further problem is that it is no longer normal in Britain, or is even in some cases illegal, to collect statistics separately for people of different races. Many of the figures cited here are thus relatively old, or are merely estimates. However, the purpose of citing data is primarily to give readers an idea of the issues in question: consequently the figures are often rounded or approximate, and meant to be taken as illustrative rather than exact.

What is an immigrant?

It would be pointless to review here the long history of transfer of individuals and groups from one political state to another. Suffice it to say that immigration is a common phenomenon. Nonetheless the concept of immigration and related terms such as "immigrant" need to be defined with a certain amount of care in the present context. The discussion in this book concentrates on "voluntary" movements, although just what is meant by "voluntary" is not completely clear since people can be coerced in a large number of ways, some more subtle than others. What is meant here is migration which takes place without legal compulsion, physical force, and the like. Watson (1977) has identified four kinds of voluntary immigrant: refugees, settlers, sojourners and "educational transients" (p. 5). Of these, refugees probably occupy a marginal position between voluntary and involuntary immigrants. Some of the foreigners who have come to Britain in the past have clearly been refugees, for example Jews from Eastern Europe who arrived here during the 1930's. However, the majority of immigrants in recent times, and especially the immigrants from the New Commonwealth on whom the present book concentrates, cannot be included in this category. Of the remaining classes of immigrants (settlers, sojourners and educational transients), it is clear that the latter two groups at least consist of people who do not plan to remain in the receiving society on a permanent or even long-term basis. Indeed, Kovacs and Cropley (1975) have argued that the truth is that very few immigrants actually plan to stay in the receiving society for the rest of their lives. This question of whether or not immigrants expect to remain permanently is of considerable importance. The problem for strangers in a strange land is that total acceptance of the ways of the new society usually requires rejection of many of the norms of the homeland. This means that incorporation into the new society normally occurs at the cost of some degree of estrangement from the old (although the extent to which this is inevitable is a debated point, as will be discussed later). Thus, immigrants who are not sure whether they will be returning to the homeland often do not know how far they should go in adjusting themselves to the receiving society. This process of adjustment to the new and estrangement from the old may not be apparent to the immigrants in relation to themselves, but it is painfully obvious to most of them if they become parents. Should they encourage their children to learn the language and accept the norms of the new society, or should they attempt to preserve the ways of the old? When the attitudes of the new society include prejudice against the old, the situation becomes particularly acute.

The phenomenon of living for a long time in a receiving society, even raising children there, but always having at the back of the mind the intention of returning home has been applied specifically to the United Kingdom by Jeffrey (1976, p. 144). She identified it as one of the factors inhibiting integration of West Indian immigrants, speaking of the effects of the "rhetoric of the return". Khan (1977) also referred to the strong expectation of returning home which exists among Pakistanis at the time they set out for Britain. To some extent this phenomenon poses a problem even for immigrants who really will be spending only a limited time in the new country, such as sojourners (for example business men, diplomats or academics whose work takes them to several different countries for relatively long periods), or what Richmond (1967) called "transilients" (people who possess high technical or professional qualifications and are willing to live, for a time at least, in any congenial society which offers them appropriate rewards for their skills and knowledge, but who move on when better opportunities develop elsewhere). However, these people can get away with making only minimal adjustments to the receiving society, and many even openly reject the lifeways of the host society in the case of their children, often going to the extent of sending them back to the motherland to be educated. The problem of immigrants, however, is that, despite the rhetoric of the return, they or their children may actually remain for a lifetime. In this case failure to adjust to the new society may have unpleasant or even severe consequences (see Chapter 5).

The United Kingdom is not the only country playing host to groups of strangers who are not clear whether they will be remaining permanently and who produce a generation of children born in the receiving society but, to some extent at least, raised according to the ways of the homeland. A notable example is the Federal Republic of Germany (Cropley, 1982) which is now host country for approximately 4.5 million foreign workers and their families (*Gastarbeiter*), including about 1.4 million children under eighteen (about 9 per cent of all children in this age group in West Germany). Many of these children were born in the Federal Republic. In theory at least, all must eventually return to their native lands (Turkey, Yugoslavia, Italy, etc.), but many will undoubtedly spend their entire lives in West Germany.

Who emigrates, and why?

Two interesting questions are which members of any particular society emigrate (for example the cleverest and most enterprising, the most disadvantaged, or some other group), and the reason why people emigrate at all, regardless of which sectors of society are involved. Rose (1969) mentions the point of view, supported by Taylor (1976), that it has been the most enterprising who have chosen to emigrate to the United

Kingdom. However, Jansen (1970) has concluded that, on a worldwide basis, there are no universal characteristics setting off immigrants as a special group. Nonetheless, the role of emigration in the society from which immigrants come exerts an important influence on who emigrates, whether or not emigrants expect one day to return to the homeland, how rapidly or extensively they adapt their ways to match those of the receiving society, which customs and values of the homeland they attempt to retain, etc. As will be seen in Chapter 4, travelling to strange lands to seek economic advancement is part of the tradition of life in both Pakistan and the West Indies, something which has important consequences for the way in which immigrants from these regions adapt to life in Britain.

The second question (the reasons for emigration) is traditionally analysed in terms of two sets of factors, "push" factors on the one hand, and "pull" factors on the other. Push factors are conditions in the homeland which encourage people to leave. These factors can include social turmoil such as war, oppression of various kinds, economic exploitation, feelings of despair or hopelessness, unemployment, starvation, and similar factors. Pull factors are the characteristics of the receiving society which encourage people to take up residence there. These may include perceived social and economic advantages, a romantic feeling that the receiving society is a land of opportunity, or even deliberate policy on the part of the receiving society to tempt immigrants to leave their homelands and take up life in the new country. This latter phenomenon, which could unkindly be referred to as the deliberate seduction of immigrants, has been relatively common in recent times during periods when highly industrialized nations have found themselves short of labour. Some countries, such as Australia, have gone so far as to set up in foreign countries networks of recruiting offices whose job is to "sell" the receiving society, and have provided subsidized passages for would-be immigrants (including Britons).

In the case of immigrants to the United Kingdom, both sets of factors have been at work. In other words immigrants have been encouraged by circumstances in their homelands and have, at the same time, been attracted to Britain. The West Indies and Pakistan, for instance have long traditions of emigration as a legitimate and accepted tactic for getting ahead in life (Taylor, 1976; Watson, 1977). In both countries lack of opportunity as a result of population pressure, unemployment, division of farms among children to the point where the holdings become too small to support a family, debt, poverty and even pre-existing uprooting such as occurred at the time of the partition of India and Pakistan, have combined with this acceptance of emigration as a social institution in such a way that it is possible to speak of emigration as a "way of life" or a local "industry", leading to the development of a "remittance economy" based on emigration (Watson, 1977, p. 7).

As the same time, immigrants have been "pulled" to the United Kingdom by the availability of jobs, as was the case during the 1950's, by a belief that Britain was the mother country and a land of opportunity, and even by long standing customs such as the recruiting of Sikhs into the British Army, or the hiring of Kashmiris by British steamship companies. The pulling power of the United Kingdom was increased by the passage in the United States in 1952 of the McCarran-Walter Act, which restricted entry to that country, as well as by the drying up of Cuba and various states in West Africa as job sources for citizens of Britain's main immigrant-sending countries. Nonetheless, a major pull factor was the United Kingdom's need of immigrant labour. This means that Britain herself contributed to the movements here of immigrants, and should not simply wash her hands of them now that their labour is no longer needed.

Historical development of immigration to Britain

Immigrants are, of course, no new phenomenon in the United Kingdom. Four hundred years ago there were 4,000 Walloons living in Norwich alone, while 80,000 Huguenots were in Britain in 1685 (Mullard, 1973). From about 1790 to 1810 a wave of Irish labourers entered Britain. About 100 years later, from the late 1800's into the early 1900's, there was a steady influx of East European Jews. More recently the United Kingdom has received groups of Poles, of whom about 120,000 came to stay during the second world war, as well as Italians, Maltese, Chinese, Cypriots, West Africans and, most recently, refugees from Vietnam. Over the years many of these groups have been the recipients of hostility to immigrants on the part of the local populace, particularly because they were perceived as contributing to the exploitation of workers by offering a pool of cheap labour or by taking jobs away from the locals, or else on straightforward racist grounds. As studies in other countries including Australia (Kovacs and Cropley, 1975) and West Germany (Cropley, 1982) have repeatedly shown, such negative reactions to immigrants are common, and are by no means confined to Britain.

Traditionally, citizens of Commonwealth countries have been in a privileged position, largely as a result of a sentimental relationship reinforced by legal and political ties, such as the continuing presence of governors as the official heads of state or the continuing role of the British Privy Council as the highest legal tribunal. There have also been strong economic ties such as trade treaties giving preference to goods from the Commonwealth in Britain, and to British goods in Commonwealth countries. Finally, but not of least importance, are cultural ties reflecting common use of the English language, mutual interest in cricket, and similar factors. In other words, Commonwealth peoples have been tied to Britain by an invisible but potent network of both *interest relations* (economic advantages, etc.) and also *sentiment relations* (shared interests, values, etc.) (Wood, 1934).

Initially, as a result particularly of a 1948 Act of Parliament, citizens of Commonwealth countries were for a number of years free to come and go in Britain, almost without limitation. Apart from people from Australia, New Zealand, Canada and the like, whose forebears had often emigrated from Britain in the first place, and who frequently regarded the United Kingdom as "home", there was a steady trickle of immigrants from Asia and the West Indies between the two world wars, consisting largely of sailors manning British ships or of former soldiers. However, Mullard (1973) dates the commencement of large scale immigration from these regions in modern times from the arrival of the *Empire Windrush* in June 1948. During the labour shortage which occurred from the mid 1950's, to the late 1960's, Britain pursued a policy of deliberately recruiting workers from the New Commonwealth: for example London Transport set up a recruiting office in Jamaica. Largely as a result, immigrants from the West Indies began arriving in large numbers from 1955 on, and from Pakistan from 1957. This means that New Commonwealth immigrants came to Britain largely in response to the local labour shortage, and with the full agreement of British policy makers.

The pattern of arrival of immigrants to the United Kingdom has been greatly influenced by a series of Acts of Parliament and associated White Papers which have appeared since the second world war. Of these, the first was the British Nationality Act of 1948 which conferred citizenship of the United Kingdom upon citizens of colonies and member countries of the British Commonwealth. Presumably this Act was intended to strengthen ties between Britain and British outposts around the world, once direct links such as rule by colonial officials had disappeared. It also clarified the position of descendents of settlers in both Old and New Commonwealth who wished to remain in the colonies, having developed strong loyalties to them, but whose British ancestry needed somehow to be recognized and whose links with the mother country needed to be made clear. It may well also have been affected by sentimental or condescending feelings that the former colonies had earned the right to be clearly British as a result of their sterling service during the war.

The 1961 Commonwealth Immigrants Act had the effect of greatly accelerating the inflow of immigrants, although its ultimate intention was to restrict immigration. In 1951 for example, there were only about 15,000 settlers from the West Indies in this country (Foner, 1977, p. 125). The number of Pakistani immigrants was even smaller. By 1961 there were approximately 170,000 West Indians and about 25,000 Pakistanis! The act of 1961, which came into effect in June 1962, imposed a quota of 30,000 immigrants per year from Commonwealth countries. It triggered a considerable rush of New Commonwealth immigrants to Britain in the eighteen months before it came into force. A White Paper published in 1965 further reduced the quota of immigrants to 8,500 per year, and imposed the requirement that would-be immigrants must possess a vocational qualification before they could be admitted.

The second Commonwealth Immigrants Act of 1968 was of particular importance in the present context. It introduced for the first time a specific, although indirect, racial basis for the regulation of immigration. The Act established special priorities for applicants with parents or grandparents born in the United Kingdom. This meant, in effect, that the descendants of Britons who had earlier emigrated to the countries of the Commonwealth could enter Britain on a favoured basis. Since the descendants of people who had earlier emigrated from Britain were virtually always white, the effect of the 1968 Act was to distinguish, for the purpose of entry to the United Kingdom, between white and coloured immigrants. The distinction was strengthened by the introduction of the concept of "patriality" in a 1971 Act.

The British Nationality Act of 1981 introduced an important principle, in that, since January 1st 1983, simply being born in the United Kingdom no longer carries an automatic right to citizenship. The effect of this, for the present purposes, is that children born to immigrants are only "British" if the parents are judged to be "settled" in Britain. Children born in Britain to parents not settled here may even become stateless, depending upon the citizenship laws of the country from which the parents come. On the other hand, immigrants who had right of abode in Britain on December 31st 1982 and were already settled here can become British citizens by registration, while the position of children of such residents is clear — they are citizens. Many people from the West Indies lost their UK citizenship when the various West Indian countries became independent. They will have to register, in some cases within five years, if they wish to become UK citizens, important for instance for passing on UK citizenship to children born here.

Despite the various Acts regulating immigration, there has been a steady growth in recent years in the number of coloured residents of this country. To some extent this has been the result of natural growth. However, there has also been a flow of new arrivals: in 1979 for instance over 40,000 new settlers arrived from New Commonwealth countries. Many of these people were admitted under regulations permitting the entry of certain groups of relatives and dependents of persons already in the United Kingdom. In the year ending Sept. 30th 1982 the corresponding figure was 30,000. Despite this steady growth, however, the pattern has not been regular. In 1972, for example, there was a net *loss* of immigrants from Pakistan.

At the present moment there are about 650,000 West Indians and about 250,000 Pakistanis in Britain. The total number of coloured residents is expected to rise to at least 3 million by the year 2000, even if there is no further immigration. There are now about 1 million coloured people who were born here and, if the prediction for the year 2000 just cited is fulfilled, in twenty years' time there will be at least 2 million such people, a large proportion of them UK citizens by right of birth. Thus, it is apparent that the coloured Britons are here to stay.

Focus on West Indians and Pakistanis

The case of West Germany which has previously been mentioned also illustrates in an international context a further important issue in discussions of immigration to Britain. Like the United Kingdom, the Federal Republic of Germany and its political predecessors has been a receiving society for foreigners for many years. Hamburg alone is reported to have over 30,000 residents who are native speakers of English. Nonetheless when Germans speak of "foreign workers", and especially when they refer to *Gastarbeiter,* it is quite clear that they are not referring to people like the 30,000 English speakers in Hamburg or the many thousand other settlers, sojourners and educational transients from Eastern Europe, Scandinavia, Japan, Iran and similar countries. In common usage, it is clear in West Germany that *Gastarbeiter* means, in the first instance, Turks, and more generally workers from Yugoslavia, Italy, Greece, Spain and Portugal, in addition to Turkey. A general expression is thus widely used by the public in a narrower sense, even if this is not strictly correct according to a dictionary definition.

In the United Kingdom an analagous situation prevails. It is necessary to face squarely the fact that in common usage the term "immigrant" means people of Asian origin (usually from the Indian subcontinent or via Africa), and of African origin (usually via the West Indies). Thus it has clear colour overtones (Verma and Mallick, 1978), since the overwhelming majority of residents of the two regions just mentioned are characterized, among other things, by having brown or black skins. In the present book, then, the word "immigrants", when used to refer to settlers in the United Kingdom, should be understood to mean people of African or Asian background, unless the context makes it clear that the word is being used in its more general sense.

Two additional terms need explanation at this point. The expression "New Commonwealth" is sometimes used here to refer to the Indian subcontinent, the West Indies, and African countries colonized by the British. It is also sometimes convenient for the sake of clarity to draw a contrast between residents of the United Kingdom who have immigrated from the New Commonwealth and those who have come from other Commonwealth countries where the majority of the population is of British or other European ancestry (e. g. Australia, New Zealand, Canada). In this case the term "Old Commonwealth" is occasionally employed. Finally it is frequently necessary to refer specifically to the most visible characteristic of the overwhelming majority of New Commonwealth immigrants, the colour of their skins, and in this case the general terms "black" or "coloured" will be employed. Although current usage of some of these terms has made them pejorative or offensive, the intention here is to achieve clarity of expression and ease of understanding, not to indicate negative values or attitudes. It is hoped that readers will understand them in this way (i. e. as aids to understanding), will appreciate that the terms do not imply any lack of respect for the people referred to by their use, and that they will be read without offence.

The present book attempts to make statements which are capable of being applied to New Commonwealth immigrants in general — indeed, in some places to immigrants in general, regardless of where they come from or where they go to. However, where specific details are required, it has not been possible to deal in detail with every specific subgroup of immigrants. For this reason, the book focuses on immigrants to Britain who came from Pakistan and the West Indies, especially where specific details are required for the purpose of the analysis contained in the text. This should not, of course, be taken as indicating a lack of interest in other groups, nor as suggesting that they are in some way less worthy of attention than the two groups upon whom attention is concentrated. The restriction of scope has been consciously adopted only as an aid to clarity, and does not imply any value judgements about any group of immigrants.

Differences among people and groups

Even when the term "immigrant" is narrowed to refer to coloured people from the New Commonwealth, the usage remains imprecise. Immigrant pupils in British schools come mainly from the West Indies, India, Pakistan, and from Africa (Townsend, 1971), although many of this latter group are of East Indian origin. Although both are Asian countries,

India and Pakistan differ substantially in culture, religion and even eating habits; indeed, the two countries have been at war with each other in relatively recent times. Immigrants from the West Indies not only differ among themselves, but are characterized by substantial ethnic, linguistic, cultural and economic differences from both groups of East Indians. Thus, it would be quite incorrect to speak of immigrants as though they were a homogeneous group.

As a matter of fact, the two groups on whom the book will focus (i. e. Pakistanis and West Indians) provide some important contrasts between groups, in addition to the general similarities they display. For example, they differ markedly in life style in the homeland, as well as in cultural history. They differ too in religious background and in mother tongue. The two groups also differ substantially in the degree to which they are accepted by the British, the Pakistanis being particularly rejected by the local population (Jones, 1977), the West Indians experiencing less success in British schools (Little, 1975) and having lower occupational status (Rutter, Yule, Morton and Bagley, 1975). For example, Rutter and his colleagues found that almost exactly half of the main bread winners in their sample of West Indian families were in semi-skilled or unskilled occupations. By contrast, 55 per cent of a sample of Pakistani immigrants studied by Taylor (1976) were self-employed. Similarly, Rutter reported that 44 per cent of West Indian families lived in houses which they themselves owned, whereas in the case of Taylor's Pakistanis, the figure was no less than 94 per cent.

As will become apparent in Chapter 4, there are certain similarities among immigrants from Pakistan as one group and also among immigrants from the West Indies as another. However, it is important at this point to stress that there are also substantial differences within groups, with the result that generalizations about "West Indians" or "Pakistanis" should be made with a considerable degree of caution. Members of both these groups differ among themselves just as individual members of any group of people differ. In addition, there are substantial differences in backgrounds, traditions, standards, norms and even language within the group labelled here "Pakistanis" and also within the one labelled "West Indians". Members of the latter group tend to identify with their island of origin, to speak a somewhat different version of the English language according to their home island, and to come from backgrounds displaying differing degrees of industrialization, again according to the island of origin. These differences are sufficiently noticable to West Indians that they tend, in Britain, to mix mainly with people from their own island and for example, to marry among themselves (Philpott, 1977).

Differences among immigrants supposedly all belonging to the same general group are even more pronounced in the case of those from Pakistan (Khan, 1977). These people come primarily from four regions, the Punjab, Sind, the North-western Provinces and Baluchistan. These regions differ not only in terrain and thus in aspects such as the extent to which they depend upon farming and the predominant kind of farming but also in religion (e. g. Sikhism or Islam) and even in language, the main languages being Urdu (especially in cities), Punjabi, Sindhi and Pushtu. Nonetheless, with the proviso that readers should bear in mind that there are substantial differences within groups, the present book will make use of expressions such as "West Indians" or "Pakistanis" in the hope of achieving appropriate generalizations. Hopefully, this will not be interpreted as indicating an ignorance of or a lack of concern for the differences between subgroups within the larger groups, or of differences among individuals within groups or subgroups.

Immigrant children

When discussion turns to children, the initial difficulty is in defining what is meant by "immigrant". Officially immigrant children are those born abroad or those born in the United Kingdom of parents who are not settled here (excluding the Irish). However, this situation leads to a number of difficulties. For example, it is possible for a child born in the United Kingdom of parents who have been here for 10 years or more to come to school unable to speak English but, despite this fact, to be officially not an immigrant. At the same time another child, born outside the country but speaking English well and familiar with British life, can be classified as a foreigner.

In theory at least, three distinct groups of "immigrant children" can be discerned. The first consists of children who arrive in the receiving society having already reached school age, the second of children who arrive during preschool years, and the third of children born in the receiving society. Thomas and Znaniecki (1958) referred to the children born in the receiving society as comprising the "second generation" while those who arrive as children were called the "half second generation" (p. 1776). According to Steedman (1979) the pattern of adjustment in the new society differs for these three groups. Those who arrive after having already reached school age in the homeland possess the habits, beliefs, customs, values, aspirations and norms of the mother country. Those who arrive at preschool age show a mixed pattern of socialization, and those who are born in the receiving society show predominantly the socialization patterns characteristic of the receiving society.

Whether this is, in fact, correct has been questioned by Cropley (1982). Nonetheless, it is clear that the background of socialization experiences enjoyed by these three groups of children differs. Cropley has also cited evidence for the existence of somewhat different patterns of adjustment and for differing kinds of problems and difficulties in the three groups. For example delinquency is more common in children born in the receiving society. This phenomenon runs counter to what would be expected from a simple classification into those with predominantly mother-country socialization, those with mixed socialization, and those with predominantly receiving-society socialization, and requires a somewhat more complex analysis of the kind developed in Chapters 5 and 6. Nonetheless, it is clear that at least these three groups of immigrant children exist (those born here, those who arrive at a very young age, and those who arrive after having commenced schooling in the mother country). Interestingly, most coloured children now attending primary schools in the United Kingdom were born here. This means that they belong to the group which Cropley (1982) has argued is in a particularly difficult position: this is because they have never had any direct contact with the society from which their parents, and even older brothers and sisters, have derived their basic values, customs, habits and norms. Thus, for them, the clash between primary socialization factors (the family) and secondary factors (the society outside the home) is particularly pronounced. This theme will be discussed in greater detail in Chapter 6.

The "problem" of immigrant children

The most striking way to refer to any social group which does not seem to fit in and which seems to call for special measures is to refer to it as a "problem". For ease of reference this approach will be followed in the present section. However, the aim here is not to isolate immigrant children by labelling them as a problem group, but rather to achieve a better understanding of their situation. According to Little (1975, p. 68) many British schools are failing to meet the needs of these children. If anything, according to Khan (1977), some schools are *causing* psychological problems for them. Thus, in a sense, it is not that immigrant children *are* the problem, but that they *have* the problem.

From a purely statistical point of view immigrant children constitute a relatively small portion of the British school population, perhaps 4.5 per cent (Bagley and Verma, 1975). Nonetheless, there are now about 450,000 immigrant children in British schools. Of these, something like 40 per cent are of West Indian origin and about 10 per cent are from Pakistan. Although these numbers are small, it should be borne in mind that the age structure of immigrant groups in the United

Kingdom differs from that of the white population. For example, whereas about 43 per cent of the latter group is aged under 30, the corresponding proportion among immigrants is approximately 60 per cent in the case of West Indians and 70 per cent in the case of Pakistanis (see 1981 census data). The census also showed that immigrants tend to have larger families. Thus, it may be anticipated that there is a large group of immigrant children not yet of school age who will be entering British schools in the next few years. It can also be expected that in a few years' time a disproportionately high percentage of young adults of child-bearing age will be of immigrant origin, and that the proportion of immigrant children in schools will, therefore, probably increase again in about twenty years' time, even without "importation" of children from abroad. In the Borough of Brent, for instance, over 60 per cent of the 3900 births recorded in 1981 were to mothers born outside the UK. This means that simply restricting the inflow of immigrants in the next few years will not make "the problem" in the schools go away of its own accord.

It is also important to note that immigrant children are unevenly distributed in Britain, with three quarters of them living in the West Midlands and Greater London (Verma and Mallick, 1978). By 1970, many LEAs had significant numbers of immigrant children, while there were schools with up to 80 per cent immigrant pupils (Townsend, 1971). In December 1972 Townsend and Brittan (1973) approached a number of schools where they expected that the proportion of immigrant pupils would be at least 10 per cent, and ascertained that 19 out of 123 primary schools for which they received information had more than 50 per cent immigrant pupils, while three out of 95 secondary schools reported a similar percentage of immigrants. The drop from primary to secondary school partly reflects the fact that immigrant pupils beyond compulsory school age stay on at school less frequently and for shorter periods. Bagley and Verma (1975) reported that by the early 1970's about 1,000 out of 34,000 schools in the United Kingdom had more than 25 per cent immigrant pupils. In two LEAs the proportion of immigrant children was in excess of

25 per cent, in five between 20 and 25 per cent, and in six between 15 and 20 per cent.

Problems of academic achievement

The actual extent of difficulties at school among immigrant children is difficult to determine. For example, as early as 1968 Wiles reported that immigrant children whose entire schooling had taken place in the United Kingdom obtained marks as good as those of non-immigrants, and Taylor (1976) drew attention to the fact that it is commonly reported that the school performance of immigrant children improves with the degree to which their education has been obtained in this country. Taylor also reported that, among a group of Asian youths, the proportion who stayed on beyond compulsory school age was considerably higher than for local children. This was true not only of those who went to selective schools, but also among those who went to secondary modern schools. It also remained true when groups were matched for socioeconomic status. However, it should be born in mind that both the immigrant and the local children in Taylor's study had poor school records. Despite these positive findings, a recent summary by Steedman (1979) concluded that immigrant children — not only in the United Kingdom but in other Western European countries as well — are generally reported to:

1. do less well in their studies;
2. be overrepresented in special classrooms;
3. leave school earlier;
4. be underrepresented in selective forms of post compulsory education.

A review of earlier studies in Britain supports this conclusion (see Bhatnagar, 1970; Christopher, 1972; Peace, 1971; Townsend, 1971; Townsend and Brittan, 1972). More recently Bagley (1979) showed that not only were both West Indian and Asian children behind English children in achievement in both English and mathematics, but that the poorer performance of the immigrant children was still present among children who had taken all their schooling in the United Kingdom: although it was true that achievement was better among immigrant children with all their education here than among those with only partial education in the UK (as reported by Wiles and by Taylor), both groups were still considerably behind local children. In 1980 a study group established by the Department of Education and Science (DES) recommended that a national survey of the school achievement of West Indian pupils be carried out since, despite widespread concern about their school perfomance, the available evidence comes from either subjective impressions of teachers and others, or from small-scale surveys. Such studies sometimes yield conflicting or contradictory data — Driver (1980), for instance, found that West Indian girls at secondary schools in socially-deprived city areas surpassed white children in achievement. Nonetheless, there is substantial agreement that immigrant children in Britain as a group:

1. have lower average marks;
2. obtain lower scores on standardized tests of achievement;
3. are concentrated in the lower ability streams where streaming exists.

In addition, Little, Mabey and Whitaker (1968) reported that school achievement among West Indian children was not only lower than that of English children, but lower than that of Asian children too. Bagley (1979) reported that West Indians did noticably less well than Asians in both English and mathematics, and Little (1975) also reported lower achievement among West Indians than among Asians. Jeffcoate (1979) mentioned a similar result in a 1973 study in Redbridge, and concluded that this finding confirmed a national pattern. A survey of school leavers conducted by the DES in 1979 in six urban LEAs supported this view: Asian pupils as a group left schools with about the same qualifications as non-immigrants, except for somewhat poorer achievement in English, whereas in the six authorities in question markedly fewer West Indian school leavers obtained five 0-Levels (3 per cent) than either non-immigrants (16 per cent) or Asians (18 per cent). Fewer West Indians passed 0-Level mathematics (5 per cent of West Indians v. 20 per cent of Asians and 19 per cent of non-immigrants), and fewer passed at least one A-Level (2 per cent of West Indians v. 13 per cent of Asians and 12 per cent of non-immigrants). This report made an important point by calling for more research into the cause of "under achievement" by West Indians, pointing out that it is not clear whether it results from general problems of social deprivation, or whether it is a direct and specific result of experiences in schools and in the community at large. A major purpose of the present book is, in fact, to develop a psychological approach capable of explaining the mechanisms which lead to the kinds of problem just discussed.

There is also evidence that the poorer achievement of immigrant children becomes more pronounced as they get older. Taylor (1974) compared the reading achievement of Pakistani and Scottish children at ages 8, 10 and 11, and found that the Asian children were on average one year behind the British children, and that they got further behind with the passage of time. Bagley (1979) cited a study with West Indian children which also showed a similar decline between the ages of 8 and 15. Furthermore, there are already significant differences between immigrant and British children at the infant school stage. Little (1975) reported differences in vocabulary and number skills even among four-year-olds. Thus, the overall picture is not only one of lower levels of attainment in English and mathematics in immigrant children, but also one in which the differences:

1. are already present at the time children start school;
2. persist during the course of schooling;
3. become more pronounced as the children get older.

It is thus not hard to see why Little concluded that the schools are not meeting the needs of immigrant children, although it is also apparent that "the problem" is not merely a question of schools, since the differences are already present at the time of starting school.

Personal problems of immigrant children

Relatively objective difficulties at school, such as lower achievement levels, higher failure rates and failure to remain at school beyond the minimum compulsory time, are disturbing enough. However, there is a second set of school problems which are, in a way, even more disturbing. These are problems of misbehaviour or maladjustment in the schools — social or personal rather than academic problems. Bagley (1975a) has summarized a number of studies of teachers' statements about the behaviour of immigrant children and has also reported a study of his own. In his own investigation he found that 49 per cent of West Indian boys were judged by teachers to be "behaviourally deviant", whereas the figure for British boys was only 25 per cent. Similarly he found that 34 per cent of immigrant girl pupils were rated as behaviourally deviant as against only 13 per cent for British school girls. (Figures of 25 per cent and 13 per cent for British boys and girls are themselves scarcely grounds for complacency, of course, but the main interest here is in the even higher figures for immigrants.)

Bagley summarized the kinds of complaint made by teachers about the behaviour of immigrant pupils (p. 289). They were described as being "restless", "squirming", "destructive", "quarrelsome", "irritable", "disobedient", "untruthful", "dishonest" and "unresponsive". Socially they were described as frequently "isolated" or else "bullying", while girls were found to be more frequently "solitary", "miserable" and "fearful". Nicol (1974) reported that behaviour disorders among West Indian pupils are usually of the "acting out" type. In other words, these children are frequently aggressive, destructive, hostile and abusive. Associated with this reported increased incidence of disturbed social behaviour is the placement of a high proportion of immigrant children in special care settings. For example, Rutter, Yule, Berger, Yule, Morton and Bagley (1974) cited a rate of 15 per cent for West Indian children born in the United Kingdom, a figure which is much higher than that for native born children. It is thus clear that the problem of immigrant children goes beyond objective or quantitative issues and is also "psychological" or "psychodynamic" in nature — it has to do with their feelings, moods, attitudes, and so on.

Closing remarks

The present chapter has sketched out the issues with which this book is concerned, especially the "problem" of immigrant children in the schools. Later chapters of the book contain a psychological analysis of this state of affairs. This analysis focuses on the development of identity in immigrant children and the effects of being exposed simultaneously to the norms of two societies — the homeland, on the one hand, the receiving society on the other.

Chapter 3 outlines the process of identity development in general terms, while Chapter 4 gives brief sketches of aspects of the Pakistani and West Indian societies which bear closely upon identity development there. These chapters are intended as background to the later analyses covering the psychological situation of immigrants and immigrant children in Britain (Chapters 5 and 6), and the implications of this situation for schools here (Chapters 7 and 8).

3

Society, Behaviour and Immigration

Societies — A systematic basis for behaviour

People do not behave randomly, nor do they react willy-nilly to every minor fluctuation in their environment. On the contrary, they tend to behave consistently, despite variations from time to time and in differing circumstances. This tendency to be consistent is so pronounced that, when people act in ways differing from what others have learned to expect of them, the others may notice this and be surprised, perhaps commenting that the person in question "must have got out of the wrong side of the bed this morning". The individual basis of this tendency to behave consistently (allowing for factors like fluctuations in mood) is usually dealt with psychologically with the help of the concept of "personality". Despite the fact that behaviour is affected by factors within the individual person, however, it is also strongly influenced by standards or norms which people share with others. For example the groups to which people belong lay down canons or guidelines for behaviour, as well as for opinions, beliefs, values, stereotypes and the like. Although the notion of "group" and the effects of groups will be discussed more explicitly on pages 49—53, an important group for the purposes of the present discussion can be mentioned here: this is the group comprised by the nation — in the present case the "British". Despite substantial individual differences among people, there are social mores, shared by most of the members of the society, which not only define proper behaviour in a wide variety of settings, but also include "correct" opinions, attitudes, values and the like.

When immigrants arrive in a new country, then, they do not encounter a neutral environment on which they can make their own impression in their own way, purely according to their interests, abilities, skills, values, hopes and plans. On the contrary, they have to superimpose themselves onto an ongoing society with its own values, customs, habits and norms. The immigrants, in their turn, do not come with totally open minds, but bring with them the mores of their homelands — as England (1929) put it, sentiments, beliefs, values, and the like are a kind of raw material for the development of cultures and social orders which all immigrants are able to carry about the world with them. Thus, one way to look at immigration and the problems which arise in connection with it is to consider it in terms of contact between two different sets of norms or mores, those brought from the homeland by the newcomers, and those of the receiving society. The fate of immigrants is largely determined by their ability to effect a compromise between the norms they bring with them and those of the receiving society, either by changing themselves or by persuading the members of the receiving society to adapt to the presence of immigrants, or a combination of both. If a condition of mutual adjustment cannot be achieved, the immigrants will remain outsiders, experiencing the consequences which are now well know (prejudice, discrimination, etc).

The portable aspects of culture which immigrants bring with them are partly a matter of rules or guidelines about "external" components of life, such as what constitutes good manners, what, when and how to eat, how to dress properly, or how to speak to a stranger. However, they also concern what might be called "internal" factors, such as values, motives, morals, aspirations and beliefs about what qualities define a worthwhile person. These internal aspects determine to a large extent how people see themselves, what kind of expectation they have of other people, what feedback they need from the society in which they live in order to maintain a sense of being a worthwhile person, and so on. Internal factors interact with external. For example, people who cannot speak the local language or do not know how to behave in everyday social situations, or who behave in ways which the locals find unacceptable (even though the strangers may consider the behaviour in question perfectly acceptable), receive contradictory or even clearcut negative feedback from other people — being called a "black bastard" would be an example of clearly negative feedback! As a result, such people often experience feelings of reduced worth, or feel angry or resentful, or experience a sense of frustration in the new society.

How well immigrants get along in the receiving society and how they feel about their experiences there is thus largely the result of whether or not immigrants and members of the receiving society agree on how to behave in certain situations, on what to expect from other people, or on what constitutes a good person. Unfortunately the information on these subjects which the immigrants bring with them from the homeland commonly conflicts in various vital aspects with what is accepted in the receiving society. The immigrants evaluate themselves and other people in terms of the standards they have learned in their original society, but these may be inappropriate or even rejected in the new society. At the same time, the locals judge the immigrants according to the standards of the receiving society. The result is that the behaviours of both groups (locals and immigrants) are determined by one set of standards, judged according to another. (This problem will be discussed in more practical and concrete terms in Chapter 6.) The mores or standards in each society and the processes and factors through which they develop are thus very important in understanding what happens to immigrants in their new lands.

National self-image

Each society has a set of ideas about itself — about the kind of people its citizens are, their main duties, which behaviours are proper and which improper, what rights and privileges each person has, what activities are moral or immoral, and many more. These ideas give rise to an image of what the members of the society are like, and thus constitute a *national self-image* or *national self-stereotype*. The national self-image may be only loosely held among members of a particular society, but in others it may be explicitly stated, for example in poems and songs, in a national theatre, in religious and folk stories handed down from generation to generation, or in the great historical events celebrated on national holidays. In some countries it may be given legal status, for example being enshrined in a constitution setting out the major values and beliefs of the people in question as they are perceived by the framers of the constitution, and thus forming the basis of the national system of laws.

Emphasis on the aspects of identity shared with other member of the society does not mean that people can be regarded as pre-programmed according to the predominant beliefs of their particular societies. In most countries there is considerable variability from person to person about details of the values and beliefs. This variability stems, to some extent, from individual factors. However, it is also true that, regardless of what official policy may say to the contrary, most societies are divided into strata or subgroups characterized by common values, attitudes and beliefs (which may differ in significant ways from the dominant ones in the society as a whole). These groups are, not uncommonly, unified by having experienced similar forms and levels of education, congregating in similar kinds of employment, enjoying similar levels of income, and having similar social status. In this case the groups form social classes. Much of the variability between people in values, norms and mores within a society reflects differences among social classes.

Frequently a particular class tends to dominate in a society and its culture becomes the "official", "national" or "high" culture. Other social groups then tend to be viewed as ignorant, deviant or wilfully out of step with what is right, and they may be stigmatized, discriminated against, or even punished economically or in other ways for their failure to conform. Each society thus has a kind of "official" picture of what its people are like, with those who deviate too strongly from this stereotype, including immigrants, experiencing negative consequences.

The modal personality

As has been pointed out, each society has its own views about good and bad, right and wrong, morality and immorality, and so on. These are given expression in the national stereotype of the ideal person, and provide standards or canons which guide each member of the society, although to differing degrees, according to the group and individual factors which have already been mentioned. In turn these guidelines or principles are converted, at the most down-to-earth level, into rules for day-to-day behaviour. One result of this phenomenon is that there is not only a high degree of uniformity of values, opinions, goals, self-image and the like within each society, but of behaviour too. When societies are examined singly this is less obvious because of the wide fluctuations about the norm which occur. However, when a society is examined from the outside it is readily apparent that, with the possible exception of small numbers of deviants, there is a central core of traits which characterize the society. These are frequently regarded by its members as defining what a truly worthwhile person is like.

This does not mean that all people in a given society are identical in their behaviour. The existence of individual and group differences has already been emphasized. Nonetheless within each society there is a central core of accepted canons, with the result that certain personal characteristics are more prominent in some societies than in others. McDavid and Harrari (1968) have used the term "modal personality" to refer to this phenomenon. The idea is that it is possible to identify "typical" ways of behaving and typical patterns of values and motives which are more frequently seen in people raised in one society than in others. Various writers have identified the "typical" Australian, the "typical" Hungarian and so on (this point is discussed in greater detail in Kovacs and Cropley, 1975). Of course this image of the "typical" member of a society, whether it is the image of themselves held by the members of the society or the image of them held by outsiders, should not be regarded as a precise description of every individual person in the society. Rather, the modal personality is a stereotype or ideal. It lacks detail, and is only a summary of the cardinal features of a society's members.

Societal norms

Certain values and beliefs seem to affect nearly all members of a society, and exert a very strong general influence. These constitute a stabilizing or homogenizing factor in the society. There are also other sets of "rules of the game" which are less universally accepted and which have a weaker influence on the behaviour of people in the society. Thus, it is possible to identify bands or zones of societal influence. At the centre is an area of clearly-defined and strongly-held beliefs and values which are common to most people in a society, with only relatively minor deviations from person to person being tolerated, and with only a very small proportion of the population rejecting them outright. In Britain the ideal of equality before the law, the belief that children should be protected, that love is the best basis for marriage, that education is a good thing, and that people can strongly influence by their own actions whether or not they are successful in life are probably all examples of this kind of core belief — not everybody would agree with all of them, but they are strongly embedded in the society, affect people's interactions with each other, underlie much legislation, guide educational policy, and modify the lives people lead.

Beyond these central beliefs and values is a set of characteristics which are less crucial but which still exert a strong influence and are widely accepted throughout the country, despite the fact that some individuals and groups reject them. The view that it is the duty of citizens to get out and vote at elections, or the idea that it is best to be married in church are probably appropriate examples. Finally come specific behaviours which define what is correct in specific settings. These may differ markedly from subgroup to subgroup within a society, as well as from person to person. In some circles in

Britain good manners require that food be eaten with a fork held in the left hand and with the tines curving downwards. In others, eating with the fork reversed would be regarded as tolerable or even normal. Similar examples would include correct behaviour on being introduced to a person for the first time, or what one should wear when going to visit friends for the evening.

Each society thus develops characteristic behaviours, attitudes, values, aspirations, expectations and habits, both of an abstract and general kind, as well as of a concrete and specific kind. They constitute sets of *norms* which guide people's own behaviour and provide them with guidelines for judging other people's. Many people are amazed or become angry when it is suggested to them that these norms are not absolute and universal truths, but rather the guidelines of a particular society or subgroup developed by the group concerned as a help in organizing communal life. Visiting foreign countries, especially those where the resemblance to the home country is low, can be a salutory and instructive experience in this regard.

The fact that each society has its own ways of doing things and that most members of a particular society conform to these norms, at least to a considerable degree, has certain negative consequences. For example, it may lead to rigidity and intolerance for strangers, or even for new ideas. Even innovative and nonconforming people tend to operate within the limits tolerated in their society. If they do not, they may be dismissed as crackpots or even be regarded as criminal or crazy. Clear and strongly held societal conventions often lead to intolerance or condemnation of those who do not observe the dominant norms. Immigrants very frequently fall into the group of nonconformers, often aggravating the situation by being highly visible or even the subjects of political and social discussion. As a result they often become the recipients of disapproval or rejection.

On the other hand there are also distinct advantages, both for a society and for individual people, in having a fairly high level of agreement on basic values, beliefs and behavioural norms. At a national level they help people to work together in order to achieve common goals. Individuals can develop a clear idea of what they can do and cannot do, what kinds of behaviour will be accepted or not accepted, what they can rely on other people to do, how they can influence the behaviour of others, what they need to do in order to "get ahead" and what they need to pass on to their children. As a result, it is not necessary to make continuous and endless decisions about everyday aspects of life, or to be in a state of continual uncertainly concerning what other people will do next or how they will react.

The existence of widely accepted norms in a society thus has the advantage that the norms render the external world orderly and understandable, and help people to plan, deal with other people, evaluate their own behaviour, and so on. In other words, familiarity with the norms of a society enables the people who live in it to go about their daily lives without having to make endless decisions about every tiny action. People who are thoroughly familiar with the way things are done in their society can get along without expending vast amounts of energy watching for tiny cues, and without stress resulting from fear that they are doing something wrong. As will be shown later, this facilitates not only social and vocational behaviour, but contributes enormously to the development of a sense of belonging and self-confidence, and to a secure identity. In the case of immigrants, however, a major difficulty stems from the fact that they are often unfamiliar with the local norms, and become, as a result, excessively sensitive to unimportant cues. At the same time, they may also be unable to provide the locals with appropriate cues themselves. Their behaviour becomes difficult to "read".

The process of socialization

It is clear that people do not come into the world fully equipped with knowledge about the norms of the society into which they are born. Newborn babies are notoriously unwilling to conform: their eating and sleeping behaviours, not to mention their toilet habits, leave a great deal to be desired! Despite this, the very infants who behave in such unsociable ways in the early years of life eventually come to accept the rules of their societies. In learning about these rules they pass through various stages and phases of nonconformity and conformity until, as adults, they themselves become guardians of the society's mores, passing them on to their own children and often becoming extremely critical of those who deviate. This process of becoming familiar with the rules of society, and even of endorsing and transmitting them, occurs at least to some degree in everybody. The mechanism through which it takes place is known as "socialization".

The process is often regarded as having two major aspects — socialization which goes on within the family (primary socialization), and socialization which reflects the influence of factors outside the family, especially school and mass media (secondary socialization). The main people who provide the primary socialization experiences are, of course, parents, as well as brothers and sisters and sometimes close relatives who form part of the family group. The main human agents of secondary socialization are playmates, teachers, other significant adults, sports heroes, and similar people. In the earliest years the child normally has very little contact with the influences outside the family and, if it is borne in mind that psychological development in the first few years is thought to be of particular importance (e. g. Bloom, 1964), it is apparent that the family has a crucial role in this respect. Schools or school-like experiences (such as kindergartens) are usually the site of the first systematic and sustained contacts with socializing influences in the world outside the family. They thus comprise, in the first years, a bridge between primary and secondary socialization experiences.

The crucial point for the present discussion is that people as a result of experience, *learn* the norms of their societies. Luria (1961) has argued that the main task children carry out in the course of psychological development is that of learning how things are done in their society or, as he put it, acquiring its accumulated lore and wisdom. To anticipate Chapter 6, most children grow up in a setting in which they learn, in the family, the basic skills (such as the language of the country in question), and basic forms of the attitudes, habits, values and the like which are predominant in the society at large. When they go to school, as well as in other settings outside the family, they come into contact with significant socialization influences which at least in a general and global way support the experiences they have already had, and help them develop the prevailing societal skills and mores which they will require if they are to function with ease within the particular society in question.

This learning of the society's norms encompasses five dimensions or systems (Triandis, 1980):

1. Relationships with the environment (that it is friendly or hostile, to be exploited or protected, etc.);
2. The subsistence system (methods for obtaining food, shelter, and the like);
3. The sociocultural system (institutions and norms outside the individual);
4. The individual (roles, values, attitudes, aspirations, etc.);
5. The interindividual system (social behaviour, child-rearing practices, etc.).

Brown and Selznick (1955) give details of what it is that people learn in these areas. Essentially people acquire:

1. Basic disciplines or patterns of behaviour through which they express feelings and impulses. These include eating habits, toilet habits and control (or expression) of emotions;
2. Necessary fundamental skills. These include as the most obvious example, mastery of the language of the society in question. They also include basic skills such as arriving regularly at work, shopping, cleaning house, and so on;

3. Appropriate social roles. These involve knowledge about how to comport oneself during contacts with other people;
4. Appropriate aspirations. People learn what they may hope to do with their lives — their "place" in society, what they are worth as human beings, etc.

These components may be arranged in a kind of hierarchy, as has been done here. In this case, the first named functions are more concrete, more "biological", more peripheral, and have less to do with what might be regarded as the innermost core of personality than later named aspects. In the case of immigrants in Britain, it is clear that difficulties arise at all four levels. The British may, rightly or wrongly, find the new-comers dirty or vulgar, ignorant of the local language, un-skilled at dealing with other people in locally accepted ways, "too big for their boots", and so on. On the other hand, the immigrants may find local food odd or even forbidden on religious grounds, the British people cold and unfriendly, and the aspirations they see as legitimate rejected by people here. A particular problem for immigrant children is that what they learn at home and what they learn in the society at large may fit poorly together, or even be contradictory, a theme which will be developed in greater detail in Chapter 6.

Socialization and group membership

Socialization cannot be understood without taking into ac-count the fact that individual people derive much of their identity from values, motives, attitudes, aspirations and skills which they *share* with other people. Not only do individuals learn things like what they may or may not do, how they fit in with others, what are reasonable goals and expectations, and the like, but, by sharing norms and mores with other people and seeing them continually demonstrated and confirmed, they receive reassurances that they themselves are "proper" people. Although it is possible to discern national norms which apply, at least to a certain degree, to an entire society, people also learn the ways of smaller segments or sectors of their society. In other words, they acquire the norms and receive feedback about the correctness of these norms not only at the level of the entire society, but also at the level of subsections of the society. These are frequently referred to as "groups".

A distinguishable group involves a set of people whose relationships with each other are organized in such a way that the set constitutes an entity with a coherent unity, even an identity of its own (McDavid and Harari, 1968). A mere aggregate of people such as would be seen waiting for trains in a large railway station (a crowd) would not normally constitute a group in the sense just outlined. Groups have three basic properties: they behave with *purpose*, having common goals and certain threats which they agree should be avoided; they have a defined set of *interrelationships* between members, and agree on the roles to be played by the various members of the group (although this may be purely informal and communicated only through patterns of behaviour); they share a set of *norms* or standards which mould the opinions and guide the behaviour of their members.

Groups may be divided into "membership" groups and "reference" groups (Newcomb, 1950). Membership groups are formally constituted (for example a sports club or a local Church Committee), but may exert relatively little influence compared with reference groups. These may be nebulously defined (e. g., the group of people who regularly and consciously support the Labour Party or the Conservative Party), but are often capable of exerting very strong influence. A second valuable concept is that of "primary" versus "secondary" groups (Bogardus, 1949). Primary groups are ".... those generating a 'we-feeling' ...." (p. 3). When people identify themselves with a primary group they become aware that some people are part of "us", while others are outsiders, "them". The family is an example of a small, primary, reference group. "The British people" is an example of a larger primary, reference group and "Christians" or "Muslims" examples of even larger ones. In all cases people can be guided by the group in their beliefs about how they should behave in many situations, what rights and privileges they have, how they stand in relation to other people, who are good and who are bad people, what it is right to do and what it is wrong to do, and so on. For the study of immigration, all three of the groups just mentioned (family, religion and nation) are of great importance.

Admittance to groups

Membership in groups can be acquired in a number of different ways. People may make a conscious decision to join a group, such as a sports club, as result of their own personal interest, through social contacts, or by being systematically recruited in some kind of membership drive. They may be coerced into joining, for example in order to improve their business, professional or career prospects. They may even, on occasion, be forced into joining a group under pain of legal, financial, religious or other sanctions. The groups may be formally defined, as in the case of a society or club, and may even be legal entities with formal rules of membership. On the other hand, they may be informal, with no clear qualifications or legal status, as would be seen in a group of regular customers of a particular pub who habitually meet in the bar in the evening and drink together. Strangers who lean on the wrong section of the bar may arouse resentment and hostility, despite the fact that they are perfectly within their legal rights, and have no way of knowing that they have transgressed against local norms.

A practical example of the importance of admission to group membership, which shows the real-life consequences for immigrants when they are excluded from key groups, is to be found in a statement issued in February 1980 by the Commission for Racial Equality. The Commission pointed out that access to many jobs in Britain is effectively denied to immigrants by certain recruiting practices adopted by some firms, possibly without deliberate intent to discriminate against immigrants. One of the criticized approaches involves recruiting by word of mouth. Firms simply rely on the members of the existing work force to pass on information about jobs to acquaintances who are seeking jobs. Where the work force is all or nearly all white, this means that job information does not reach coloured immigrants unless they happen to be members of key groups in which the white people with the job information are also members, such as the ones consisting of drinking companions, team mates, family friends and the like — an uncommon state of affairs. Some firms also recruit through particular schools which recommend only white candidates, possibly "innocently" as a result of the fact that they do not have any coloured pupils to speak of, or because crucial teachers know only white children well enough to feel confident about recommending them. Finally comes the practice of recruiting through unions where, apart from any possible deliberate prejudice, the simple problem of lack of contact between union officials and immigrants may mean that only Whites are recommended. In all three methods of recruitment the effect is not infrequently denial of job opportunities to immigrants. This results from the fact that the immigrants do not move in the circles where the necessary information is available — they are not members of the key groups in the British society.

Of course, it is also possible that discriminatory job practices have been adopted by some firms with deliberate intent to discriminate. A 1980 "test" conducted in Nottingham by the Commission for Racial Equality, as reported in the daily press in November of that year, suggested that many firms are guilty of racial prejudice: A White, a West Indian and an Asian with equal qualifications applied for the same 103 jobs. The White was offered an interview in all 103 cases, whereas both the West Indian and the Asian were offered interviews in about half the cases. Since the number of interviews offered the white applicant was so much higher, despite equal job qualifications, and since the number of interview offers was almost identical for both coloured applicants, it was concluded that prejudice against coloured people, regardless of ethnic group, had been at work. However, a simple attempt to explain all problems of immigrants by accusing the institutions and individuals of the majority culture of deliberate, conscious, racial prejudice is, from the standpoint of the present book, neither constructive nor helpful. The aim here is to promote insight into the psychological mechanisms which lead to the various categories of reaction which have been observed, not to apportion blame or call for enforcement of "desirable" behaviour by commissions or other watchdogs.

The legal or formal criteria for membership in a group need not coincide with the subjective feeling of belonging to that group or with acceptance by the group's members as one of them. The situation is made more complicated by the fact that some immigrants, as in the case of Pakistanis and West Indians in Britain, are highly visible because of their skin colour. When one of the norms of substantial segments of the majority society is uneasiness or mistrust, even outright rejection and hostility towards coloured people, legal status as a UK citizen is unlikely to gain them admission to local subgroups. Successive governments in Britain have struggled for a good 20 years with the problem of developing formal criteria (legislation on immigration and citizenship) which are capable of dealing directly with the fact that citizens of the Old Commonwealth are technically foreigners in Britain, but frequently have a strong "we-feeling" in regard to the United Kingdom, and are readily accepted by British people, whereas increasing numbers of coloured immigrants are technically entitled to reside in this country, or are even citizens, but are rejected as fellow countrymen by substantial segments of the population and may feel themselves isolated and alienated from the British society. One nettle which very few lawmakers are willing to grasp is that most Old Commonwealth citizens are white, whereas most New Commonwealth citizens are coloured.

The role of language

One obvious phenomenon in psychological development is the acquisition of language. As children, or for that matter adults, learn the ways of a society, they acquire skill in the use of the society's language. Language as a phenomenon is sometimes regarded as essentially a communication device which is neutral with regard to the content of the communication, in something the same way as the meaning of this sentence is independent of the make of typewriter on which the words were originally typed. However, there has been increasing recognition in recent years that the medium and the message are not independent of each other. An interaction exists between language, socialization and personality development — in other words, language is an important element in psychological development, and the mother tongue is a "significant factor in personality" (Egger, 1977, p. 3).

Language is most often thought of in terms of its role in cognitive functioning — writers such as Vygotsky, Piaget and Bruner have all emphasized the role of language in the emergence of thinking. In other words, language is not simply a neutral device for expressing ideas, but an important factor in the forming of ideas, even more, a phenomenon without which thinking as we know it could not exist. According to Vygotsky (1962) there are forms of languageless thought such as are seen in young children. There are also forms of thoughtless language, again as seen in children and babies who, for example, make use of rudimentary forms of language to express emotions such as rage or fear, or for social purposes such as attracting the attention of other people or indicating recognition of members of their families.

Adult humans also use language in these ways. However, there is an important difference between adults and babies. Adults are able to blend or join language and thought, with the result that a new kind of thinking emerges which is qualitatively different from the forms of thinking seen in young children. This fusion of language and thought, which results from the process of cognitive development, permits abstract thinking. It is also important because it frees thought from dependence on momentary states or immediate environmental events. It permits planning, deriving abstract laws of cause and effect, suppressing momentary impulses in the interest of intangible rewards, making use of abstract notions such as "nationhood", and has many similar functions. As Regan and Cropley (1964) showed, the linguistic conventions of a society even shape the way in which people conceptualize time and physical space.

All three of the theorists mentioned at the beginning of the previous paragraph have traced out the sequence of steps or stages in the transformation of thinking with the development of language, each developing his own description of the process. Although there are some differences in the details of their findings, all three share the view that language is crucial for freeing thinking from domination by momentary and fluctuating concrete stimuli, making it stable, abstract and flexible. Thus, all three approaches emphasize that the acquisition of language is not a mechanical process similar to, say, learning to type, but a major element in cognitive growth. Far from being a neutral tool like a typewriter, language is an active guiding influence which is indivisibly associated with the process of thinking.

Language is now also widely recognized as an important element in the process of socialization, as well as an important outcome of this process. It is very largely through language that parents, siblings, other adults, teachers, playmates and the mass media communicate information to children about what is right, what is wrong, and so on. The effectiveness of language partly results from its abstractness. It is much easier to use words to warn children of the probable consequences of behaviour which the parents know is dangerous than to allow them to injure themselves, even though they may profit from the experience. However, language is far more than a substitute for physical action. As Luria (1961) pointed out, attaching a verbal label to a real object does more than provide a way of referring to it in its absence. The word "tunes up" whole classes of reactions to the object, links it with other objects having certain things in common, and suggests appropriate behaviours. The label "cup" or its equivalent in any other language, changes the "meaning" of a particular object, predisposing speakers of that language to treat the object in certain ways. These ways are, of course, the responses which the society regards as correct for a cup.

These responses are dependent upon the particular society's notions of the general properties of cups, or whatever happens to be the word in question. Thus, the language sums up the culture's notions of what goes with what, how various objects should be treated, and so on. The history, values, and folk ways of a society in which the word "girl" was closely related to the word "slave" could, for example, be readily conjectured, as could the consequences in that society of being female. In this way, then, language may be seen as the mirror of a culture and its history, as well as the vehicle of a set of cultural "rules" for how to treat objects and events encountered in life.

Language also plays an important role in transmitting from generation to generation information concerning what are good manners or proper behaviour, or even rational thinking. It is not merely that this information is passed from person to person using language as a convenient shorthand or substitute for actions, but that the information is stored in the form of language. Anderson and Cropley (1966) have suggested that this is done through the transmission of verbal "stop rules". According to this point of view, people regulate their behaviour according to their society's norms by formulating and storing verbal statements, which they can reproduce upon request, which consist largely of injunctions not to do certain things. Hence the label "stop rules". This suggests, of course, that a major aspect of socialization is the learning of how to restrict or limit behaviour, language functioning as an internal mechanism for blocking or inhibiting proscribed behaviours. Schubert (Schubert and Cropley, 1972) has proposed that the degree of acquisition of the capacity for "verbal regulation of behaviour" is a major indicator of intelligence or mental growth. In addition to social and intellectual functions, language also plays a role in what Titone (1978) called "ego-dynamic" aspects of psychological functioning. Language is important in individual people's feelings of belonging and competence, in their understanding of what is going on around them, in their system of values, in their attitudes, in their ability to feel and express emotions, in their unconscious and subconscious life, and in their ability to form and express wishes. Thus, language is an important aspect of each individual's personal identity.

Recognition of the close link between language and identity is of particular interest for the study of the adjustment of immigrants. It is quite clear that acquiring the standard form of the official language of the receiving society is a crucial prerequisite if immigrants are to make a successful adjustment to the new society. On the other hand, acquiring mastery of the new language is not simply a matter of learning a new technical skill, to retain an image introduced earlier, analogous to learning to type instead of write in longhand. Especially if acquisition of the new language is seen as the first step in losing the original language, achievement of mastery over the language of a receiving society may be an event of profound psychological significance to immigrants. It may even be seen as the first step in rejecting the original homeland, and may consequently be resisted, consciously or unconsciously, by immigrants themselves or, in the case of children, by their parents.

Implications for studying immigration

Each society has its own norms which provide members of the society with guidelines about how to behave, what to wear and eat, and so on, as well as about what they may reasonably hope to achieve, what rights and privileges they have, and many more. These norms include information about what good and bad people are like and what kinds of deviation from the local norms are tolerable. People thus learn what is right and what is wrong and where they fit in, who they are and what kind of person they are, as a result of participating in the life of a society — in other words they acquire a self-image or identity. The norms are learned through exposure to socializing agencies, especially in the case of children, family and school. A major mechanism in this process is the mother tongue. Not only does a particular society provide its members with information about their rights and privileges and the like, but it also offers them opportunities to test and confirm the correctness of these standards, as well as reassurance that other people feel the same, for instance through contacts with various kinds of groups whose members share values, motives, beliefs and standards, and through what is depicted in the mass media.

The process of socialization is a common aspect in the backgrounds of both immigrants and members of a receiving society. However, the details of the information acquired during socialization differ enormously from society to society. The different societies differ in what are seen as desirable behaviours, acceptable motives, the right kind of personal traits, and so on. Thus, immigration involves contact between two sets of norms, those of the sending and those of the receiving society. Members of the two groups of people involved (immigrants and locals) both believe, with differing degrees of rigidity, that their norms are correct, those of other societies incorrect. Disapproval may be expressed by saying that immigrants are "dirty", "immoral", "excessively materialistic", "atheistic", and many more.

Although the locals are subjected to a questioning of their own standards by the newcomers, the relationship between groups, both in simple numerical terms and also in terms of factors such as the distribution of power, is usually such that the strongest negative effects are experienced by immigrants. By definition, the ways of the receiving society are "correct", those of immigrants "foreign". The result is that immigrants are cut off from the reassuring feedback that their society has previously offered, feedback which has in the past tended to confirm their beliefs, standards, values, motives and the like, but which now contradicts what has previously been learned, since the receiving society teaches, if anything, that what is done in other countries is wrong by virtue of being foreign. As a consequence immigrants, as they come more and more to accent the norms of the receiving society, frequently experience a state of uncertainty or even outright self-rejection.

Chapter 4 describes some of the most salient aspects of life in Pakistan and the West Indies from the point of view of norms, in order to make the nature and extent of this clash between societies clearer. Chapter 5 then shows what typically happens when societies come into conflict as a result of immigration, illustrating the discussion with examples from recent events in Britain. Chapter 6 relates the discussions in the present chapter and the next two chapters specifically to the case of immigrant children, again concentrating on West Indians and Pakistanis.

4

The Homelands: West Indies and Pakistan

As was pointed out in Chapter 3, adult immigrants bring with them to the new country a set of beliefs, values, cultural skills, ambitions, etc. which they have acquired in the homeland. These help them to understand who they are, what is expected of them, what they may hope to achieve, and so on; adjustment to the receiving society is largely a matter of finding some form of compromise between these norms and those prevailing in the new land. According to their age, children also arrive in the new country at least partially equipped with a set of norms: even children born in the receiving society (i. e. children having no direct personal experience of conditions in the homeland) are affected by the norms of the society from which their parents come, for instance because these largely determine the rules of life to which the parents adhere as they raise their children (see Chapter 6 for a more detailed discussion of the role of the norms of the homeland in interactions between immigrant parents and their children). This means that the rules of the game prevailing in the original homeland continue to play an important role in the lives of immigrant children, regardless of where they were born.

The important point for the present chapter is that the adjustment of immigrants to life in a receiving society is greatly affected by values, attitudes, habits, norms and similar aspects of identity prevailing in the homeland — Khan (1977) for instance, has drawn attention to the importance of such factors in immigrants to Britain, stressing that they have an important influence on the speed and kind of adjustment which people make to life in this country. As Steedman (1979,

p. 260) put it, the "degree of cultural distance from the host culture" is a major factor which modifies the adjustment of the immigrants: attitudes, values and habits learned in the homeland cannot, in many cases, simply be shrugged off in favour of those of the new society, while it is also often difficult for immigrants who have been raised according to a different set of norms to identify "right" and "wrong" behaviours, sort out appropriate cues, decide what is essential, what unimportant, etc.

In short, then, the adjustment of immigrants in Great Britain is affected by the norms they acquired in the homeland. Understanding the process of adjustment to Britain and, for the present purposes, the difficulties which arise during this adjustment, thus requires an understanding of the "way of life" of Pakistan and of the West Indies, and especially of the crucial differences between the norms of these societies and those of Great Britain. The purpose of the present chapter is to provide an overview of these two sending societies, with special emphasis on factors such as family structure, social relations, attitudes to school, and the like. A major difficulty in any such discussion is that of simply repeating stereotypes, or even of reinforcing prejudices. It is thus important to emphasize that generalizations made in this chapter (or in others, for that matter) are not meant to be seen as exact descriptions which accurately describe in detail every individual Pakistani or West Indian — on the contrary, individual immigrants vary as much as Britons differ from one another — but rather as tendencies or inclinations, or sets of events which occur more (or less) frequently than in Britain, or where the "average" state of affairs is somewhat different from what is seen in this country.

Although it has already been pointed out that not only people who actually grow up in the homeland but also those who are born in the United Kingdom are affected by the norms of the society from which their parents come, this point is of such importance that it needs to be discussed separately and in greater detail. Young immigrants who shrug their shoulders and say that the way things are done in the homeland is irrele-

vant to their lives, since they were born in Britain, see this country as their home, have no intention of returning, and have no interest in the old ways are, nonetheless, in most cases also affected by the clash of norms which is the subject of the present book. In other words, the values, attitudes, habits, customs, symbols, etc. of the homeland still play a role in their lives, even if they are unaware of it. This is because the process of acquiring an identity during childhood and early adulthood is affected by not one but by two major sources of information: not only by socializing agencies in the society, but also by the blandishments, model behaviour, and the like, of parents, other family members and other adults. Indeed, since the family is the dominant influence in the early years of life, the norms of those who provide early child rearing are a decisive influence in personality development. For this reason, the place where the parents learned their particular set of rules of the game continues to be important, even for those whose secondary socialization is dominated by the norms of the receiving society. To relate this specifically to the present book, the way of life of Pakistan and the West Indies exerts, through the parents and other members of the immigrant community, an important influence on the lives even of youngsters born in Britain.

Pakistan

The first thing which should be emphasized in a discussion of the background of Pakistani immigrants to Britain is that they constitute an extremely heterogeneous group. For example, people regarded in Britain as Pakistanis may speak Punjabi, Sindhi, Pushtu or Urdu. There may even be small numbers of "Pakistanis" who grew up in Africa, coming to Britain after the 1968 exodus, or in the West Indies. As result of the division of the Punjab between India and Pakistan, some "Pakistanis" may actually be Sikhs, who may or may not regard themselves as primarily Pakistanis. Despite these difficulties, an attempt will be made here to sketch out a general overview. The people referred to hereafter as "Pakistanis" come from a group with a long tradition of emigration to Britain, for instance as a result of service in the Army or in British steamship companies (see Taylor, 1976). This tradition has largely economic roots: in 1975, for instance, a remittance of £ 10 sent home by a Pakistani working in Britain would have yielded in that country the equivalent of a month's pay (Jeffrey, 1976). Emigration is thus a kind of local "industry" in this region: in 1977, for instance, a Trade Deficit of about $ US 1,500 Million was largely offset by remittances from abroad totalling about $ US 1,000 Million. One result of this long tradition is that Pakistani immigrants can be expected to be characterized in host societies by diligence and financial prudence (Taylor, 1976), an expectation which is largely borne out by practical experience, but which may be one of the sources of the particular dislike of Pakistanis evinced by some Britons.

The traditional way of life in Pakistan has been influenced over the years by a series of important events which mean, among other things, that it can by no means be regarded as universal or unchanging. Among these events have been, in the political domain, the ending of colonial rule and the subsequent upheavals of partition; in the economic area, the increasing introduction of foreign manufactured goods and the development of an industrial economy; in the social domain extension of the franchise to the population in general and drastic changes in land-ownership laws. These events have also been accompanied by a process of internal immigration, in which rural residents have moved in increasing numbers into the cities (see Khan, 1977, for an extended discussion). Important recent changes in life in Pakistan include the increasing availability of industrial work, and the extension of education to much larger proportions of the population, especially the acceptance that education is also suitable for girls. Related to this last phenomenon is the emergence of greatly increased contact between boys and girls, with a subsequent erosion of the system of arranged marriages, although this should not be taken as suggesting that this system has disappeared or that very clear parental guidance in this domain is not still the normal state of affairs, even in Britain.

Geographic and historical overview

Pakistan has four main geographical-political regions: the Punjab, Sind, the Northwest Frontier, and Baluchistan (Khan, 1977). The locations of these regions are shown in Figure 4.1. Parts of the Kashmir are also administered by Pakistan, the whole region being widely regarded as part of Pakistan and the subject of a long-standing dispute with India. The population of about 80,000,000 occupies a territory of about 800,000 square Kilometers, the northern regions of which are mountainous, the southern containing large fertile plains. The major cities such as Karachi (three and a half million inhabitants) and Lahore (about two and a quarter million) support a sophisticated cultural life for the educated well-to-do. Nonetheless, Pakistan is still essentially an agricultural country, and about 55 per cent of the populace lives in rural regions. Farms in the north tend to be relatively unproductive with the result that they remain small and poor, but the south contains many more-prosperous farmers. Rural Pakistanis mostly live in villages with between, perhaps, one hundred, and several thousand residents. The main agricultural products are wheat, rice and cotton, while a good deal of livestock is also raised. Among the major industries is the production of textiles, a fact which, along with the prevalence of cotton production, perhaps helps to account for the frequency with which Pakistanis in Britain make their living in various branches of the textile and clothing industries.

At the time of independence from Great Britain in 1947 Pakistan became a separate country, initially consisting of an eastern and western half. In 1956 the country became a republic. Since independence it has been greatly troubled by problems of an organizational, economic, religious and political nature, including the ongoing disagreement with India over Kashmir, which has already been mentioned. These difficul-

Figure 4.1: Pakistan, including the four provinces and principal cities. The inset shows its geographical relationship to India.

ties have sometimes gone as far as civil war and war — in 1971, for instance, East Pakistan seceded to become Bangladesh, a set of events which culminated in a war with India in 1971/72. In 1972 Pakistan withdrew from the British Commonwealth, partly as a result of ill feeling over the events surrounding the founding of Bangladesh. In 1977 Martial Law was imposed, and in September 1978 General Zia ul-Haq became the country's president, after the failure of the disputed 1977 elections to bring stable government.

Religion

No fewer than 97 per cent of the population of Pakistan are Muslims, and the country is now officially an Islamic Republic. This religion is characterized by a very clear set of laws which define an ethical code of conduct, not only in religious, but also in day-to-day behaviour. A second important characteristic of Islam is that it is not a local or regional religion, but has a worldwide following. By contrast with Hinduism, which is much more abstract, or with Sikhism which partly has the nature of a Punjabi national freedom movement, Islam is more "portable" and more "practical". What this means is that Muslim immigrants in Britain tend to be more "culture-bound". Taylor found, for instance, that more Muslims than Sikhs or Hindus in a group of Asian immigrants which he studied could read their mother tongue, claimed to be devout, reported that they had only Muslim friends, and maintained religious customs such as avoiding the eating of pork or the observing of Ramadan. Islamic culture thus affects everyday life, even in the new society, and encourages maintenance of a certain degree of exclusivity.

Without entering into a detailed theological discussion, it is worth pointing out that the guiding values of Islam include: following the precepts of the Koran and, in particular, submitting oneself to the will of god; faithfully and loyally carrying out one's duties (e. g. as a child, as a villager, as a Muslim, etc.); standing by one's kin; looking after old people and, in the case of women, remaining modest and chaste. As Khan (1977) pointed out, rural Pakistanis still accept these basic values — the result is considerable anxiety for them when they come into contact with competing norms, even within Pakistan itself, as occurs, for instance, when rural people move into the cities. Although it could be claimed that similar norms to the ones just listed prevail in Great Britain, it is readily apparent that a large proportion of the population gives them only lip service, and that the pious Muslim would quickly become aware of the existence of a different set of values in the British society.

Social structure

The Pakistani society is characterized by a kind of cast system, although it cannot be compared in strictness or importance to that which prevails in India. It remains true, however, that there is a tendency for sons to enter their father's occupation, and for marriage to take place within one's own caste. In the rural regions it is possible, according to Khan (1977), to distinguish between two "social classes", the one consisting of landowners, the other of those who do not own land. Landowners, of course, farm their land, while non-landowners work as craftsmen, artisans or labourers. Small landowners may also take part time work as labourers, off their own property.

An important factor in interpersonal relations in Pakistan is the kinship or "brotherhood" system. Kinship is based on descent from a common male ancestor, although it is also strengthened by, or even independently conferred by such factors as coming from the same village, or belonging to the same occupational group. A person's kin may be expected to provide "services" — advice, financial help, suitable mates for one's children, a kind of welfare system for the weak or needy, etc. According to Khan (1977), despite various kinds of social changes and the emergence of new economic activities such as paid labour, former villagers retain their ties with their home locality, even after they have emigrated to Britain. They tend to think of the original village as their home, even if they never return, and tend to regulate their friendships in Britain according to kinship and geographical bonds of brotherhood. The importance of these considerations for life in Britain is discussed in Chapter 5, for instance in relation to the tendency of Pakistani immigrants to form ghetto-like communities which are often regarded by the British as a sign of outright hostility directed at them.

Family life

A typical Pakistani family, especially in rural settings, usually consists of six to eight people coming from three generations — grandparents, sons and unmarried daughters (married daughters go to live with the family of their husband), and finally children of the sons (Khan, 1977). A rural family typically lives in its own small house, built around a courtyard. Property is held in common by the family unit, so that a kind of pooling of resources occurs. Nonetheless, the senior male in the family unit is the head of the family. Decisions are made on a communal basis, in the sense that they are discussed among the members of the family, but the eldest male has the final say. Each position in the family has a kind of hierarchical rank, with well-defined rights and duties. There is thus a pattern of subordination of the individual to the group. One aspect of this is to be seen in the strong emphasis on respect for one's parents, a second in the area of choosing a bride. Marriage is regarded as more a social duty than a romantic adventure and, although the situation is not as pronounced as in the case of Hindus or Sikhs, the young Pakistani man is expected to discuss his desire to marry with his family, and to make necessary arrangements through the good offices of his mother (Levi, 1957).

In keeping with the communal family structure which has already been described, child care is shared by the adults in a family group. It tends to be relaxed and affectionate rather than authoritarian. Children learn the norms of family life largely by observing adults. By an early age they are aware of their responsibilities to the family and to their kin, and are expected to behave consistently with these responsibilities, within the limits imposed by their youth. By puberty, sex roles in work and social behaviour are already well established.

Schooling

At independence Pakistan inherited the British system which had been introduced with colonialism. By 1972, however, a new educational policy had been introduced, stressing among other things, universal, compulsory elementary education, the increasing of adult literacy, and the implementation of an agricultural-technical bias in education, in keeping with the country's needs. A five-year plan for 1978—83 emphasized the need to increase educational expenditures in order to achieve these goals. According to this plan, universal elementary education was to be reached in 1983 in the case of boys, in 1987 for girls.

Education is highly valued by Pakistanis, even by peasants who may themselves have had little or no schooling. In particular, it is regarded as the pathway to a better life. One consequence of this attitude is that a high proportion of Pakistani children in Britain stay on at school even after passing the age for compulsory attendance (Taylor, 1976). Schools in Pakistan are authoritarian, in the sense that the teacher is regarded as an infallible source of knowledge, highly disciplined in the sense that children are expected to work hard and behave well, and extremely standardized (uniform lesson plans, set texts, etc.). Decisions in the school domain are made by experts, and there is no role in the system for parents. Once again, the reaction of many Pakistani parents to British schools (see later discussions in Chapter 6) needs to be viewed against this background. An important element of the Pakistani school curriculum is the role of "Islamiat" — the study of Islam, which is seen officially as the core of schooling, since it provides the rationale or philosophy of national life.

Emigration

As has already been mentioned, Pakistan is a country with a long tradition of emigration, both internal and external. In recent times, the target countries have included Mauritius, South and East Africa, the West Indies, Fiji, Guyana and the Middle-East, as well as Great Britain. The two world wars had an effect on emigration patterns from Pakistan, especially in view of the tradition of soldiering in some groups. After both world wars some Pakistani soldiers stayed on in the United Kingdom, while during and after the second world war there was also a tendency for merchant seamen to settle in the United Kingdom.

The purpose of emigration is frequently not merely personal advancement, but also improving the lot of the family, even of the village. The importance of remittances has already been emphasized by setting their value against the total Trade Deficit. In a society with an average annual income of perhaps £200, even small sums by British standards make an enormous difference to a family's standard of living. As a result, the actual cost of emigration is often financed by the brotherhood or the family. At the time of leaving, the Pakistani emigrants typically assume that they will be returning — in fact, emigrants are "required" to return, in the sense that this is "correct" behaviour, and failure to return constitutes a serious breach of duty. Thus, esteem and status norms in Pakistan dictate that emigrants to Britain should return to their native village, even if only from time to time. Although, as will be discussed more fully in Chapter 5, Pakistani emigrants are ambivalent in their attitude to British life, this expectation that emigrants will return means that members of the family and kin who remain in Pakistan hear a great deal about life in Britain, much of it positive. Returning emigrants tend to create an extremely positive picture of life in this country, naturally emphasizing their successes in the new land. To those who remained at home they seem to return possessed of considerable wealth and a great store of worldly wisdom (see Khan, 1977, for a detailed discussion).

Once again, as will be seen more fully in Chapter 5, these aspects of what might be called the "psychology of emigration" in Pakistan cast considerable light on both the behaviour of emigrants once they have arrived in Britain, and on the kinds of problems they may be expected to have in adapting to life in this country and in bringing up their children here.

The West Indies

Just as in the case of Pakistan, one of the first things which needs to be said about the West Indies as an immigrant-sending region is that there is a great deal of variability from island to island. For instance, West Indians tend to identify with a particular island, not only before they emigrate, but also after their arrival in Britain. This tendency extends to the formation of friendships in Britain, and even to choice of mates, although it cannot be seen as constituting a rigid kinship or cast system, being based as it is mainly on shared acquaintances and relatives, shared interests and loyalties in the West Indies, and so on. The importance of the norms of the homeland for West Indian immigrants in Britain has been emphasized by Philpott (1977): even in this country their behaviour is frequently affected by a system of social sanctions based on the values of the homeland. News about unacceptable behaviour not only travels back home, where it affects the good name of emigrants and of their family, but it also circulates in the United Kingdom, as a result of the system of informal bonds linking immigrants from the same island and the same locality. A further interesting aspect of the situation of West Indians in the West Indies is that they are newcomers even in that group of islands. As Hiro (1971) put it, even in the homeland West Indians are still "searching for a culture and an identity".

Geographical and historical overview

The West Indies, as the term is used here, refers to a group of some 14 or 15 independent or semi-independent states in the Caribbean region, ranging from Guyana in the south-east to Belize in the north-west. Their distribution in the Caribbean Region is shown in Figure 4.2. The islands were originally colonized by either the British or the French, starting in the early 17th Century (St Kitts, for instance, was colonized by the British in 1623), all of them eventually coming under British control. The present populations are largely descended from Africans brought to the region as slaves, although the proportion of Africans in the populations, as well as the ethnic origins of other groups, varies from state to state. On

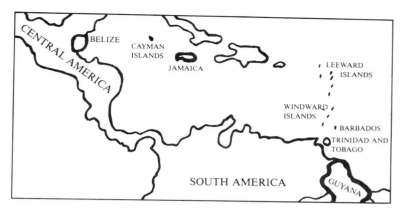

Figure 4.2: The Caribbean Region from Belize in the northwest to Guyana in the southeast. Individual states in the Leeward and Windward Island chains are not shown.

Trinidad and Tobago, for instance, although still the largest single group, Africans constitute under 50 per cent of the population, and are scarcely more numerous than East Indians. One consequence of these historical and geographical conditions is that, although English is the official language of all of the West Indian islands, on some of them the ordinary day-to-day language of many of the inhabitants is a form of French patois (e. g. Dominica, St. Lucia). Another is the variability in the dominant religious groupings on the various islands: although all are nominally Christian, Protestantism prevails on most, whereas on St. Lucia or Trinidad and Tobago there are high proportions of Roman Catholics.

Another astonishing aspect of the region is the enormous variability in the size of its member states: Jamaica, with a population of about 2.2 million, is comparable to such relatively well-to-do nations as New Zealand, whereas Anguilla has a population of fewer than 10,000, Montserrat of well under 20,000! Although all West Indian states have democratic forms of government, they vary in political orientation, ranging from the strongly socialist-oriented Grenada, with close ties with Cuba, to the (under the present administration)

US-oriented Jamaica, which is reducing its links with Cuba. Common to the West Indian islands is a heavy dependence on agriculture and tourism as major sources of income, although some also have well-established mining (e. g. Jamaica) or manufacturing sectors (e. g. St. Vincent and the Grenadines), while Trinidad and Tobago has considerable income from its oil industry.

Social structure

Basically there are four colour groups in the West Indies (see Foner, 1977) — Whites, people of mixed origin, East Indians and Blacks, although the proportions of these groups in the population differs from island to island. There is also a kind of class system, with large landowners comprising the upper class, small landowners the intermediate class, and labourers and tradesmen the lower class. These three classes partly correspond to the colour system just mentioned, in that large landowners tend to be white and poor labourers black. A high proportion of black West Indians consists of villagers who make their living as small farmers or labourers. The villages have little industry, with the result that unemployment is high. In the context of the present book, the term "West Indian immigrants" may be taken as referring to Blacks, usually from a rural background, and usually descended from Africans who were originally brought to the islands as slaves. One important phenomenon in West Indian society is the position of women. Whereas in Pakistan they are traditionally subservient to men, there is a tendency for West Indian women to have equal status and even to play the role of head-of-the-household. This position is also borne out by the fact that on some islands the literacy rate is higher among females than males, as well as by the high proportion of young women among emigrants to Britain.

Family life

There is a certain degree of dispute about the "typical" features of West Indian family life (see Philpott, 1977). Nonetheless, the remarks which follow are true for a considerable proportion of West Indian immigrants to Britain. Families tend to be loosely structured and unstable. West Indian men often marry very late, but may have several "affairs" before marrying, with resulting illegitimate children (see Foner, 1977). Among the group sending the most immigrants from Montserrat, for instance, 50—60 per cent of all children are born out of wedlock. Children of these unions are normally raised by their mother, single mothers thus being relatively common. There is often only superficial contact between parents and children, especially between fathers and their children. Unmarried children typically stay at home, so that there is a considerable degree of fostering and informal adoption of children, the grandmother, for instance, often looking after her unmarried daughter's children. Despite what has just been said, there is a well-developed idea of kinship and of obligation to kin (e. g. Philpott, 1977). There is also a well-developed sense of obligation to the family, and an acknowledgement of the importance of helping the family. One practical manifestation of this is the tendency for those already in the United Kingdom to help finance the journey of other kin who also wish to come to Britain.

As has already been pointed out, children are often raised in a household containing three generations, and headed by their maternal grandmother. There is a tendency for attitudes about how children should be raised to be "Victorian" (see for instance Fitzherbert, 1967), despite the looseness and informality of relationships between children's parents. Children are expected to contribute to the family's work and to the raising of money. They also help with manual work such as caring for animals, gathering wood or water, collecting fruit, running errands, or helping with household chores such as laundry, cooking or looking after the babies (Philpott, 1977).

Social norms are often communicated by stories about legendary "good" sons or fathers, or, of course, "bad" ones. A "good" person would, for instance, be one who had emigrated to Britain and had subsequently sent large amounts of money or major gifts to those left behind in the homeland. A "bad" person would be one who failed to live up to the obligation to look after those left behind in the West Indies. This form of socialisation not only has the effect of transmitting an image of the good person to children, but also tends to promote acceptance of emigration as a desirable activity, which can lead to high prestige if the emigrant is successful and fulfils all obligations.

Schooling

Education has high prestige in the West Indies. It is seen as the pathway to jobs, status, power and material possessions, and is regarded as making it possible to transcend skin colour. Despite this, Foner (1977) has pointed out that West Indian immigrants typically expect to receive less education in Britain than local children — an expectation which possibly accurately reflects practical experience in this country (see Chapter 2). As might be expected, there is considerable diversity in educational provision on the islands. On Barbados, for instance, there is free, compulsory education up to the age of 16, and a literacy rate of 97 per cent has been reached. Jamaica has free primary education which is compulsory in many regions, and a literacy rate of 90 per cent, while Grenada has free, compulsory education until the age of 14, Trinidad and Tobago from 6—12. On the other hand, St. Vincent and the Grenadines has free, non-compulsory primary education, but attendance is low with, of course, a relatively low level of literacy in the population. Despite the provisions and attitudes to education which have just been mentioned, until about 10 years ago access, especially to secondary education, was frequently restricted by the existence of fees. This means that many adult immigrants who come to Britain from the West Indies have had only restricted schooling.

Emigration

As is the case with Pakistan, the West Indian islands have a tradition of emigration — going to another country to work is regarded as normal (Foner, 1977; Philpott, 1977). The United

Kingdom is by no means the only country to which West Indians have emigrated in the course of the present century or, indeed, to which they continue to emigrate. Until the 1952 McCarran-Walter Act many of them went to the United States. However, the passage of this act, which limited immigration into the United States from the West Indies, led to a considerable upsurge in the numbers going to the United Kingdom. The pioneers who came to this country in the early 1950's came, of course, to a new and strange society in which they did not have the comfort of kin who had already settled here. However, they soon encouraged others to come after them, and even provided financial support to finance the cost of emigrating to Britain, in the phenomenon referred to by Foner (1977, p. 126) as "chain migration".

Among the chief characteristics of West Indians who emigrate to Britain are that they are mostly of rural origin, that they are mostly what might be called "working class" people, that a high proportion of them are young, many of them being under thirty at the time of emigration, and that they tend to stay in Britain for a long time. Despite what has just been said, West Indian emigrants to Britain tend to have a-bove average education and skills, by West Indian standards. Early emigrants from Jamaica, for instance, were largely skilled or semi-skilled workers, although more recent emigrants have included a higher proportion of unskilled and agricultural workers. One interesting aspect of West Indian emigrants which distinguishes them from those from Pakistan is that there is a high proportion of young women among them. Not infrequently, children may be left behind (for example with their grandmother), the intention being either to return or to bring them to the United Kingdom at a later date.

The "migrant ideology" (Philpott, 1977, p. 115) which has already been mentioned, means that leaving the children behind is not necessarily a sign of irresponsibility: the emigrant is expected to send money back for the care of those left behind, and the children of those who fulfil this obligation, especially those who are able to do it on a generous scale, may even gain considerable status because their parents are "good" people, fit to take their place among the legendary heroes of the West Indies. This leaving of children to be cared for by their grandmother is also a sign of a further important phenomenon among West Indian emigrants: both Philpott (1977) and Foner (1977) have drawn attention to the fact that virtually all of them intend eventually to return home. In fact, Foner (p. 137) refers to Jamaican immigrants as being "dominated" by the idea of returning home. Despite this, as Philpott pointed out, only about 20 per cent actually do return.

Closing remarks

Despite the enormous differences between individuals and groups which have already been referred to, it is possible to make a number of generalisations about emigrants from Pakistan and the West Indies. Both groups come from societies in which emigration is perfectly acceptable as a way of achieving economic advancement. Both groups are strongly affected by the expectation on the part of many individuals that they will eventually return home (even if this expectation is not actually fulfilled). Contacts with the mother country are maintained through informal kinship and locality bonds, which persist even after settlement in the United Kingdom. These bonds mean that a large proportion of immigrants remain aware of their obligations to people in the homeland who do not emigrate, and that they continue to be affected by the norms of the societies from which they came. In other words, their behaviour continues to be regulated by the norms of the homeland, even though they are living in a society with many different traditions and usages. As will be discussed in more detail in Chapter 6, this continued link with the homeland has special significance for immigrant parents. For instance, the very agency which they revere and accept as an instrument for getting ahead — the school — is also the place where their children are exposed to norms which often conflict with those of the homeland, with the result that it may be regarded by parents as simultaneously desirable and undesirable.

5
Adjusting to a new society: Process and problems

Discrepancies in norms

In each society people learn norms concerning, on the one hand "social relations", on the other "culture" (Foner, 1977, p. 122). In other words, each society has rules for getting along with other people, a set of beliefs and values, and a system of symbols for dealing with the external world. An important part of these norms consists of guidelines for establishing what constitutes a "good" person: these make it possible to judge both other people and oneself. Each society also provides its citizens with feedback or confirming information which tends to show that the norms they espouse are "correct". Parents, teachers, playmates and friends, authority figures, religious leaders, as well as the various media, all accept basically similar norms, and offer various kinds of rewards and punishments for adherence or non-adherence to them.

This means that the behaviours people emit and the ways in which they evaluate themselves and others depend, to a great degree, upon the mores or standards of the society in which they grow up. However, societies differ from each other in what is regarded as appropriate both in social relations and also in areas such as culture, religion, values and attitudes to life. Unfortunately from the point of view of relations between immigrants and members of receiving societies, there is a strong tendency for each society to imagine that its norms are the "right" ones, and that deviations from them are stupid, ignorant, cantankerous or even hostile. This is scarcely surprising, since it is hard to imagine a society which deliberately maintained standards it regarded as wrong. Interestingly, it appears that even members of underprivileged groups such as the poor, or social outsiders such as habitual criminals, tend to accept the basic norms of their society, and may even be proud of being "good" or "loyal" members of the society, apart from certain relatively superficial deviations which have led to poverty or incarceration.

Immigrants to Britain bring with them norms acquired in the homeland. What they encounter when they arrive is an ongoing society which is just as convinced as are the immigrants that *its* ways are the correct ones. The immigrants may find the local language incomprehensible or, as has already been mentioned in discussing West Indians in Britain, they may find that their version of the English language differs noticably from the ones accepted in this country. The immigrants are also confronted with local habits and customs of which they know little or nothing, some of them attitudes to the immigrants themselves. Social customs may differ markedly from what has always been correct in the past, particularly puzzling for immigrants to Britain who believe that they are arriving in "the mother country".

The discrepancies between the norms which the immigrants bring with them and those which are accepted in the receiving society range from disagreements on broad and abstract matters, such as the properties of the ideal person, to lack of agreement on small day-to-day actions which most people carry out automatically without even being aware that they are emitting complex and highly-organized behaviours. A simple example at the most down-to-earth level involves the correct actions to pay for a ride on a bus, or to use a public telephone. This clash between norms is the crucial dimension around which the analysis in the present book of relations between West Indian and Pakistani immigrants and the British society is organized.

Reaction of the locals — stereotyping

The people who are natives of the receiving society are, for their part, confronted by strangers who appear to be ignorant of many of the most basic social decencies. Not only may they speak the local language in an unintelligible way, but they may display ignorance of how to carry out even simple everyday acts, may wear odd looking clothes, and may eat strange or offensive foods. Not infrequently, the locals' awakening awareness of the strangers in their midst may be accompanied by annoyance, impatience, hostility and rejection. Failure to conform to the local way of doing things is frequently assumed to reflect either ignorance or rejection, and often provokes calls that the immigrants either fit in or get out. The locals belong to various groups in their own society, and frequently become acutely aware of their membership in these groups, and indeed in the nation as a whole, as they become more aware of the presence of immigrants. Differences between themselves and the immigrants are assumed to indicate defects in the background or character of the newcomers, who are then often assumed to be lazy, dishonest, unreliable, stubborn, antisocial, dirty, and so on. Particularly where the strangers are clearly visible, for example in Britain because they have black skins or wear different kinds of clothing, a strong sense of separateness from the newcomers may develop among the locals, along with well developed negative feelings towards the outsiders. The situation is thus ripe for the emergence of a strong ingroup-outgroup or "we"-"they" relationship.

Typically this tendency for relations between locals and immigrants to develop into an ingroup-outgroup relationship is accompanied by the phenomenon of stereotyping. Certain characteristics are thought to typify the outgroup in question (in this case West Indian or Pakistani immigrants), and individual members of the group tend to be treated, not in terms of their personal characteristics as individuals, but in terms of the properties attributed to the group to which they belong. To a certain extent, stereotypes may be seen as serving a useful purpose: they function as a "short cut" (Lindgren, 1969, p. 239) which makes it easy for the members of one group to become aware of the salient features of another. However, it is also apparent that stereotypes are often grossly inaccurate or wildly exaggerated. For example, Collard (1970, pp. 82—85) reported that immigrants in the United Kingdom are stereotyped as "dirty", "immoral", "obsessed with sex", "badly educated" and having "a chip on their shoulder", while they are said to "smell" and "urinate in the streets". Studies reported in Verma and Bagley (1975) showed that among senior secondary pupils in Britain both West Indians and Pakistanis were overwhelmingly stereotyped in negative ways, for example as "untrustworthy", "mean" and "dirty". In one study involving free descriptions of Pakistanis and West Indians written by 14- and 16-years-olds, for instance, about 70 per cent of the adjectives used were clearly negative, only about 17.5 per cent positive. Pakistanis received even more negative stereotyping than West Indians. The fact that these kinds of perceptions by the British largely reflect stereotyping rather than accurate surveys of reality is shown by the fact that immigrants in Britain tend to have an unusually high level of home ownership, to have high levels of personal savings, to be against trouble making, and to be hard working people (Collard, 1970; Taylor, 1976). Although there are undoubtedly some who are lazy, dirty or immoral, this is not true of all of them.

Prejudice

Although there are obvious disadvantages for both groups, the fact that people tend to identify themselves as members of a group and to treat members of other groups according to preconceived stereotypes is not necessarily always a bad thing. As has already been mentioned, for example, it is probable that stereotypes contain at least a germ of truth (e. g. Berry, 1970). However, when the nature of the stereotypes is overwhelmingly negative, what happens is that individual members of a relatively weak outgroup which is on the receiving end of negative stereotypes are "punished" for their membership in that group. This becomes a serious problem when the outgroup depends upon the good opinions of the ingroup for successful adjustment to the society in which both groups live. If the ingroup which possesses the negative stereotypes against the outgroup is powerful — numerically, culturally, economically, or all three — a predisposition on the part of its members to react in a negative way to members of the outgroup is referred to as "prejudice".

Of course, it is also prejudice for a small and weak group to react to members of large and powerful groups in preconceived negative ways. Thus, it would be possible to speak of "prejudice" on the part of immigrants to Britain against the majority society, a theme which will be discussed more fully later. However, prejudice is not normally regarded as a problem where the groups concerned are of approximately equal strength or where the group which is on the receiving end of the prejudice is so powerful that it suffers only minimal negative consequences as a result of the prejudice. Thus, it is customary in the United Kingdom to be more concerned about the prejudice of the British against immigrants, and to be less concerned about prejudice of immigrants against Britons. Indeed, at the present moment the consequences of prejudice flow largely in one direction; immigrants suffer considerably as a result of prejudice against them, but the consequences of immigrants' prejudice against the majority society are, as yet, barely noticable.

Prejudice against foreigners living in Britain is no new phenomenon. In the late 1500's Elizabeth I observed that there were too many black people living in England, and commanded that such people should be removed. As a result, many were actually deported. In 1903 a Royal Commission reported reservations about the growing number of immigrants to Britain. More recently, successive governments have wrestled with the problem of dealing with the growing number of immigrants in this country, usually in terms of how to limit or restrict their numbers or even of how to persuade them to leave.

As has already been mentioned, this problem takes on a special form in the United Kingdom because of the fact that the immigrants are nearly all black or brown in skin colour.

Although experience in countries such as the Federal Republic of Germany or Australia shows that colour differences between members of the receiving society and the immigrants are not necessary for prejudice to occur, the phenomenon in Britain has become a question not merely of prejudice but of racial prejudice as well. Thus, many British people complain that white people are being put out of work by Blacks, or that it is impossible to go shopping any more without being jostled by coloured people. Power (1979, p. 45) cited a survey in Britain showing that about half of the respondents were particularly opposed to coloured immigrants, and complained for example that they "brought in disease" or were "dirty". Similarly, nearly half of the respondents thought that a coloured worker should be laid off before a white one. Thus, prejudice against immigrants in Britain is a more complicated phenomenon than in some other immigrant-receiving societies.

The whole question of prejudice poses a special problem for the British. The society greatly stresses fair play and equal rights. At the same time, there are strong ingroup feelings and a strong sense of the superiority of the British people. In the case of reactions to coloured immigrants, these two dominant values conflict with each other: the "attitudinal paradox" (Jeffcoate, 1979, p. 19) of the British is that their norms require them to be friendly and helpful to immigrants, while at the same time encouraging them to entertain feelings of superiority or even hostility towards outsiders. One of the consequences of this paradox is the phenomenon which has already been mentioned — the flat denial on the part of some liberal-minded and well intentioned people that prejudice exists at all.

Discrimination

Prejudice would presumably be of minor significance if it had no practical consequences. However, it is unfortunately true that prejudice in Britain is linked with significant and systematic disadvantages suffered by immigrants. Whether or not prejudice directly causes these disadvantages is not clear: this point will be discussed more fully in a later paragraph.

One major disadvantage suffered by Pakistani and West Indian residents of the United Kingdom is that they are concentrated in residential areas where they often live in cramped, shared accommodations lacking some of the basic amenities such as a bathroom or separate living and sleeping quarters. They usually live in areas where the housing is deteriorating and where other services such as public transport, entertainment, shops and the like are either lacking or are themselves of deteriorating standard. It is thus probably appropriate to speak of a form of residential discrimination against immigrants in Britain. Details and surveys of this problem have been reported by many writers including Nicol (1971, 1974), Rutter, Yule, Morton and Bagley (1975) and Jones (1977). Taylor (1976) has made the interesting point that even among a sample of Pakistanis whom he studied, where the rate of homeownership stood at over 90 per cent (by contrast with an overall rate in the city in question of 28 per cent), the overwhelming majority of their houses were located in the poorest and most rundown sections of the city.

A second kind of discrimination suffered by immigrants in Britain involves the jobs they obtain. Generally they are concentrated in the lowest paid jobs involving the dirtiest, most boring, or otherwise most unattractive kinds of work. Foner (1977) has discussed in detail the problem of job discrimination against West Indians. Taylor (1976) referred to an earlier study which showed that 34 per cent of Asians questioned believed that they had experienced job discrimination, for example by not being promoted when they had deserved it, preference being given to a white Briton. In his own study Taylor found that a similar proportion of his respondents (32 per cent) believed that they had experienced job discrimination. However, it is very important to notice that no fewer than 50 per cent reported that they had *never* experienced job discrimination. An interesting statistic in this regard has been cited by Power (1979, p. 111). He reported that unemployment among West Indian school leavers is double the national average. The Nottingham study of discrimination in employment already referred to earlier is worth mentioning again here: when a Black, an Asian and a White with equal qualifications applied for jobs with 103 firms, the white man was offered an interview in all 103 cases, whereas both Black and Asian were offered interviews in only about half the cases. This situation was attributed by the Commission for Racial Equality to racial prejudice on the part of employers.

Despite what has just been said, it is important to ask whether the kinds of disadvantage suffered by immigrants which have just been described can always be attributed solely to discrimination, or whether they reflect other, perhaps quite understandable factors. For example, claims by immigrants that they have failed to get ahead in their jobs as a result of discrimination and not of their own shortcomings could be explained as a rationalization used, consciously or unconsciously, as an alibi to explain away their own inadequacies. Certainly, anecdotes involving coloured immigrants who have reflexively accused policemen of harassing them because of racial prejudice, or teachers of giving them poor marks because of prejudice, ignoring the fact that the police officers or teachers in question were themselves coloured, lend some credence to the idea that crying racial prejudice is a convenient way out for some immigrants. On the other hand, Taylor (1976) has pointed out that there is evidence that immigrants do not necessarily seize upon discrimination as a rationalization of their problems and that, indeed, many specifically deny that it has caused them any serious difficulties. In any case, considerable care should be exercised before reflexively explaining away all unpleasant experiences by invoking racial prejudice.

Concentration of immigrants in undesirable jobs could be seen as a logical consequence of their lower levels of attainment and their failure to achieve academic qualifications, phenomena which have already been described in Chapter 2. After all, it is the common (although not universal) lot in the British society that persons with the lowest levels of educational achievement occupy the lowest rungs of the vocational ladder. To be set against this is the fact that there are grounds for believing that even immigrants with relatively good educational achievements frequently fail to obtain employment of an appropriate kind. Ballard and Ballard (1977) give the example of Asian university graduates. Although there is now a not inconsequential number of Sikhs who possess degrees from universities in the United Kingdom, a high proportion of these graduates are unemployed. This finding suggests that the relationship between qualifications and employment may be negatively biased in the case of immigrants, even though it is sadly true that underemployment is also the fate of many white Britons.

Racism

When discrimination is related to differences between groups which include differences in skin colour, the issue becomes one not merely of discrimination against one group by another, but of racial discrimination. In treating relationships between coloured immigrants in Britain and the local populace as, to a considerable degree, a question of racism, Jeffcoate (1979) has distinguished between "institutional racism" and "individual racism". In schools, institutional racism is seen in curricula which are totally oriented to the needs of middle class white children, and in textbooks which present coloured people as being inferior. Institutional racism is also seen in practices which confine immigrants to certain kinds of job, or restrict their opportunities for advancement. Individual racism takes many forms but is clearly seen in verbal abuse of individual immigrants, harassment in the form of derogatory remarks, physical bullying, painting of slogans on immigrants' fences, vandalism against their property, or even assaults upon their person. As Jeffcoate emphasized, these two forms of racism interact: individual racism is a reflection of institutional racism but, at the same time, is an indispensable prerequisite for it.

A further useful concept is that of "official racism" (Power, 1979, p. 48). Official racism is clearly seen when immigrants suffer legal disadvantages as a result of which they have fewer rights than the members of the receiving society. This legal discrimination may be relatively minor: for example, in many receiving societies immigrants pay income tax in the normal way, but are denied the avenues available to the locals for expressing their opinions about the ways in which their taxes should be spent, for instance by voting. In other countries, the situation is more severe: for example, immigrants may be permitted only to work in certain areas or even only for specific employers, with subsequent increased prospects for exploitation of various kinds. Even in countries such as the United Kingdom, where discrimination of the forms just described is at a relatively low level, official racism may take the form of a failure on the part of public officials to help immigrants exercise the rights that they have, or a failure to protect them from certain disadvantages to the fullest degree possible under the law. It may also take the form of harassment by officials which falls within the legally permitted limits, but lies outside the accepted norms of the society. Many immigrants claimed that this kind of racism was being exercised against them by the British police, for instance through the use of their power to stop and question suspicious persons (the infamous "SUS" Law). Whether or not these charges are well-founded, it is apparent that the whole area of official racism is one in which there is great potential for discrimination against immigrants. Even differences in the amount of time well-meaning public officials put into reviewing the cases of claimants of different races could lead to widespread discrimination against immigrants, possibly without conscious awareness on the part of the people committing the racist acts.

Assimilation

There is a strong tendency for people to believe that, apart from the tolerable levels of variability which have been discussed in Chapter 2, substantial differences between individuals and groups within a society are undesirable, and that so-

cieties should strive to achieve the highest possible level of ho-
mogeneity in order to avoid conflict (Dalby, 1972). Indeed,
the phenomena of stereotyping, prejudice, discrimination
and racism which have just been discussed make it clear that
the presence within a society of groups of strangers not infrequently leads to unpleasant consequences for those people.
This is particularly the case when they are readily identifiable
(i. e. are highly visible) because of different physical appearance or different patterns of behaviour. As a result, there is
considerable pressure on immigrants, not only in Britain but
in other countries too, to adjust or adapt themselves to the
ways of the receiving society, in order to avoid or minimize
the disadvantages which have just been described — in other
words to assimilate.

The basic concept of assimilation is easy to understand. It
involves the process of adjustment of the immigrants to the
new society. However, this process is complex in nature, involving, on the one hand external adjustments, on the other
internal ones (Taft, 1966, p. 2). External aspects of adjustment to the receiving society include factors like mastery of
the local language and adoption of local dress and work habits. Internal aspects involve adoption of the values, standards
and mores of the new society. A truly assimilated immigrant
would thus not only conform to the external norms of the receiving society, but would actually replace internal norms
(values, motives, image of the "good" person, etc.), developed during socialization in the mother country, with those of
the receiving society. In other words, a person assimilated to
this degree would not only conform to the local norms, but
would actually believe in them. Truly assimilated immigrants
would, in fact, actually prefer the ways of the receiving society to those of the homeland.

In moving towards this state, which may well never be
reached by more than a handful of immigrants, various stages
of adjustment can be discerned. Taft (1966, p. 10) has distinguished between "primary integration" and "secondary integration". At the first or primary stage of adjustment to the
new society immigrants still experience homesickness and ad-

here substantially to the norms of the mother country, especially in the internal sense, despite the fact that they may be beginning to feel at home in the receiving society. In the stage of secondary integration the immigrants reach a high level of adjustment to the receiving society and of estrangement from the norms of the mother country, even if they are not consciously aware of the fact. This adjustment may include habitual use of the language of the new country, achievement of a certain degree of vocational integration, social contacts with locals, and acceptance of local norms.

It is very important at this point to notice that the achievement of a high level of internal assimilation or secondary integration into the receiving society frequently involves abandoning habits, standards, values, even self-image and identity developed in the mother country. It is not clear to what extent estrangement from the norms of the mother country is essential to adoption of those of the receiving society. For example, Smolicz (e. g. Smolicz and Secombe, 1977) and Putniňs (1976) have both argued that forms of adaptation of immigrants to receiving societies which do not require estrangement from the norms of the mother country are possible. Khan (1977) and Ballard and Ballard (1977) have made a similar point in discussing the adaptation of coloured immigrants to the British society, describing a form of integration which results in people who are capable of functioning successfully in two societies.

However, it is apparent that the achievement of such a bicultural assimilation will be, if not impossible, at least much more difficult under certain circumstances and in certain areas of adjustment. For example, where the internal norms which define the properties of a worthwhile person in one society directly contradict those of another, it is difficult to see how acceptance of the standards of the new society could be achieved without enormous conflict. In a similar vein, where the norms of the receiving society include specific rejection of the habits and values of immigrants' mother countries, or even hostility towards their skin colour, it seems likely that the process of assimilation to the receiving society will be accompanied by serious internal strains. Kovacs and Cropley (1975) have argued that it is necessary and inevitable that assimilation to a new society will involve some degree of estrangement from the old. They called this process of estrangement "alienation".

It is thus not clear whether or not it is possible for immigrants simultaneously to espouse the norms of two societies. It may be that adjustment is usually accompanied by a certain degree of loss of the ways of the mother country, a loss which is to some extent compensated for by partial acquisition of the ways of the receiving society. This is essentially the thesis of the present book. However, what is clear is that the circumstances under which adjustment to the receiving society occurs will help to determine how much discomfort is experienced by the people making the adjustment. At the one extreme are conditions of assimilation according to which immigrants must abandon the ways of the homeland swiftly and completely, totally and unconditionally accepting those of the host country. At the other extreme are approaches which permit maintenance of the norms of the mother country, or even accept the possibility of some degree of adjustment of the receiving society, rather than demanding that the immigrants make all the adjustments.

The first approach requires the "unconditional surrender" (Kavass, 1962, p. 64) of immigrants to the receiving society. As Taft (1953, p. 46) pointed out, this would require that they became "emotionally dead" to their homelands. It is not surprising that research on immigration has shown that where this pattern of assimilation, referred to as "monistic assimilation", prevails, immigrants have been observed to display certain kinds of resistance. One such pattern of resistance has been the substitution of mere external adjustment while retaining the internal norms of the homeland. Another approach has been withdrawal into immigrant communities which have functioned almost as ghettoes. The phenomenon of resistance to assimilation in Britain will be discussed more fully in a later section.

Other writers have stressed the need for some degree of give on the part of the receiving society. Taft (1953), for example, called for the development of "shared frames of reference", with the norms of the receiving society adapting in such a way as to incorporate key aspects of the immigrants' norms. However, it was apparent to Taft that the greatest degree of change would be made by the newcomers. Saunders (1980, p. 33) has called for "mutual accommodation" in Britain, emphasizing the need for a "multicultural" approach to assimilation of immigrants, based upon the notion of a mutual "social accommodation". An example in Britain of such an adjustment would be recognition that the English spoken by about 60 per cent of West Indian immigrants is a legitimate instrument of expression rather than a sign of linguistic and mental retardation or social deviance.

Assimilation of immigrants in Britain

Although the main interest of the present book lies in problems or difficulties associated with the presence of coloured immigrants in Britain, it must be made clear that a substantial degree of assimilation has been achieved by both groups and individuals. Immigrants have made a contribution to British life merely by being in this country, their "exotic" clothing brightening the appearance of the city streets, their accents adding a new dimension to the sounds in shops and on the streets. Staid British cricket crowds are now noisier and more excitable than they were 20 years ago, a development not greeted with approval by all lovers of the game. Even the smell of spices is now a new but common phenomenon in some areas. Mosques and temples give new shape to skylines, and the sight of Muslims praying in parks gives a sense of being in a more varied society than that of a few years ago.

Apart from their contribution to the general atmosphere, especially in London, Birmingham, Bradford and the like, coloured immigrants have also made many concrete contributions to British life which are proof of the cultural and economic assimilation achieved by some of them at least. In the case of British food habits, for example, Pakistani restaurants are now commonplace, even in relatively small cities, penetrating as far as the north of Scotland. In some cities, school meals now include curry as well as traditional English dishes! The effect of West Indian Reggae music is, of course, well known. In the fashion world too, immigrants have exercised an influence, more than half of all the shops on mod Carnaby Street now being run by Asians. In academe many immigrants, especially Asians, are to be found among teaching staff.

Two areas of particular potential for influencing British society where immigrants are now breaking in are politics and sport. Although still relatively poorly organized as an effective political lobby, possibly because of a desire to avoid becoming involved in controversy which might only make their situation worse, immigrants have made notable breakthroughs, such as the election in 1979 of Mr. Jagdish Rai Sharma as mayor of the London Borough of Hounslow. Of great interest here is the fact that only a small proportion of the electors were Asians. Since Viv Anderson broke into major English soccer, other coloured immigrants have achieved prominence in this sport, while Daley Thompson has become a major figure in British athletics. Breakthroughs of these kinds seem likely to do much to improve acceptance of coloured Britons, and also to foster their belief in their own ability to make good in this country.

The influence of coloured immigrants on occupational patterns in Britain is well known. Without their labour London Transport could not function, while the same is true of the British hospital service. However, immigrants have also begun to break through in other areas. It is now possible, for example, to receive a ticket for overparking from a turbaned Sikh! In the Metropolitan Police, at present, there is only a small number of Asian or West Indian officers, despite the obvious importance of integrating immigrants into the force. Nonetheless, Mr. Ronald Hope, London-born of Guyanan parents, was promoted in 1979 to Inspector in the Metropolitan Police, the first person of coloured immigrant background to achieve this rank. Thus, immigrants are beginning to break away from the pattern of being confined to certain industries and holding only the least desirable jobs in those industries.

Alienation in Britain

Despite what has just been said, it is clear that immigrants are still suffering severe estrangements from the British society. They experience higher unemployment and, apart from a small number of cases, are confined to unattractive jobs which local workers will not take. They are the victims of job discrimination which takes various forms, including the discrimination in recruiting which was discussed in Chapter 3, as well as the form experienced by Mr. Sohan Singh Sagu in Leeds, where it became necessary for him to work behind a wooden screen to protect himself from the spiteful acts of his white workmates. These forms of alienation in work are in addition to straightforward cases of discrimination through refusal to hire or promote immigrants on the grounds that Whites should be given preference. Sometimes employers are forced to adopt such measures by pressure from the work force.

Occupational alienation can also be looked at in a more global way. For example Taylor (1976) found that 40 per cent of the fathers in the families he studied had been farmers in Pakistan, while 22 per cent had been shopkeepers, and only 22 per cent had been employees, whereas most of them started in Britain as employees and all lived in a city. Thus, the transfer to the United Kingdom had, at least initially, been accompanied by a drastic change in the kinds of job a number of these people worked at, as well as, for many, a switch from rural to urban living. (Subsequently, however, a large number of the members of the Taylor sample had succeeded in re-establishing themselves in occupations involving various forms of self-employment, although the farmers had not been able to obtain farms in Britain.)

Of more central interest for the present discussion are forms of estrangement or alienation which are of a more "internal" kind — forms involving values, morals, ambitions, self-image, and the like. When they leave their homeland and enter the receiving society, immigrants are, to put it dramatically, torn away from the system of norms and supporting influences comprised by the society of the mother country. The extent to which this experience, frequently referred to as involving "culture shock", is unpleasant or even destructive is usually thought to depend upon the *magnitude* of discrepancies between the ways of the homeland and those of the receiving society, on the one hand, on the *kinds* of discrepancy (the areas of life in which they occur), on the other (e. g. Steedman, 1979). In other words, the shock experienced by newcomers depends both upon quantitative factors and qualitative factors. A brief outline of some of the salient aspects of life in Pakistan and the West Indies has already been given in Chapter 4. Readers' familiarity with the norms of British society will, no doubt, quickly suggest many contradictions between life in this country and that in the West Indies and Pakistan.

Even in the subjective domain of feelings, identity and the like, alienation may have a concrete base, or concrete consequences. For example aspects of the self-image based on physical characteristics may have to be adjusted. A girl who is considered to be fair-haired in Pakistan or the West Indies is likely to find that she is regarded as dark in Britain. A tragic but compelling example of discrepancies of this kind and their sometimes appalling consequences was reported in the daily press on April 4th, 1979. An inquest into the death of an eight-year-old Pakistani boy after a simple operation revealed that he had bled to death. The problem was that his brown skin concealed from nursing staff the pallor associated with loss of blood. To the staff his skin colour appeared rich or full when, by the standards of dark-skinned people, he was very pale.

Rejection of British ways by immigrants

In both objective and subjective domains, alienation from British life among immigrants does not reflect solely rejection of immigrants by the locals. It also reflects, to some degree at least, an unwillingness on the part of some immigrants to accept certain aspects of British norms. In the case of Pakistanis, for instance, Jeffrey (1976) has pointed out they consciously reject many aspects of British life. They find the British, judged by the standards of Pakistan, immoral and heartless. Young girls wear revealing clothing, go to dances, and even drink alcohol. Marriage is frequently marked by infidelity, and divorce is common. Parents do not supervise their children properly, and fail to teach them the right ways to behave. Children, for their part, do not respect and obey their parents, and neglect them wickedly when they grow old. At a more concrete level, many Pakistanis regard British food as terrible! West Indians also experience discrepancies between the mores of the homeland and those of Britain, discrepancies which do not always reflect positively upon life in this country. Actually, as Khan (1977) has pointed out, immigrants experience ambivalent attitudes towards life in the United Kingdom. They may see its people as immoral or cold and rejecting, but they are aware of Britain's potential as a land of opportunity, and they desire to make a success of themselves in the new country.

The ghetto phenomenon

One effect of the kinds of estrangement or alienation from the British society, both tangible and intangible, which have just been discussed is a tendency for immigrants to cluster together in ethnic communities. These develop into something approaching ghettoes. West Indian immigrants, for example, very frequently live close together in suburbs where people from home are highly concentrated, even retaining village and kin relationships from their own islands, and tending to marry people who were neighbours on the home island (Philpott, 1977). Both Khan (1977) and Jeffrey (1976) have discussed this phenomenon as it applies to Pakistanis. Jeffrey has made the point that their tendency to live close together in certain localities is usually assumed to be thrust upon them as a result of discrimination in housing. However, she stresses that the tendency to take over rundown sections of the cities may, to a substantial degree at least, reflect the voluntary choice of the Pakistanis. They often prefer to live in central sections of the cities, and not infrequently deliberately seek out cheaper accommodation because they want to send a high proportion of their income to Pakistan instead of using it to pay interest, and thus like to pay off mortgages very quickly. Jones (1977) has supported this view, pointing out that it is logical for immigrants to seek out areas where housing is plentiful and cheap, and subsequently for newcomers to join their friends who are already established.

In a study of Pakistanis in Britain, Jeffrey (1976) found that the immigrants in her group did not really want to assimilate into the British society. Relationships with British life were almost nonexistent. The immigrants carried on social contacts and leisure activities with members of their own group. They had their own newspaper, radio and TV programmes, and maintained their own food habits. There was little intermarriage with British people and, where contacts did occur, the tendency was for the Pakistanis to try to convert the British to their ways. On the other hand, Saunders's (1980) summary of a number of investigations of young Asians in various British cities led him to conclude that the people in these studies *did* want to leave the ghetto and become members of the majority society, the linkage with their neighbours being acceptance by all parties of the values of the traditional "solid" working class (regardless of skin colour). Especially in the case of Pakistanis, there was a marked tendency to identify with the values of the appropriate social class in the British society, rather than with those of the homeland. However, this was accompanied by mixed feelings — a simultaneous desire both to escape from the norms of the Pakistani subgroup and, at the same time, to hang on to certain of its desirable aspects. This condition of simultaneously rejecting something while, at the same time, wanting it, will be referred to later as involving a "double bind" (see Chapter 5), especially when no satisfactory compromise offers itself.

Taylor (1976) has specifically analysed the role of ethnic communities in the kind of terms adopted in the present book. He pointed out that immigration involves a "social and psychological dislocation" (p. 165). However, living with other immigrants makes it possible to recreate something of life in the homeland, and thus provides (p. 165) "psychological reassurance". As Dahya (1974) put it, mixing with their fellow countrymen is a positive and dynamic way for immigrants to deal with the strangeness of the receiving society. It helps to keep alive the traditions of the homeland, affords entry to an existing status structure, helps in the achievement of financial security, provides some degree of protection from exploitation, and helps to overcome anxiety.

Any discussion, such as the one in the preceding few paragraphs, which draws attention to the positive or constructive aspects of clustering together of minority group members, immediately runs into objections from people who think either of apartheid or of ghettoes, such as Soweto or Harlem. The purpose of the present discussion is not to recommend ghettoes as the primary way of handling relations between majority societies and minorities. However, it is important to realize that the mere tendency of immigrants to live in close proximity to each other, or even to prefer cheap accommodation, need not necessarily reflect hostility to the dominant society or, to take an even more negative interpretation, an actual preference for run down localities — proof of the accuracy of stereotypes of immigrants as dirty, dishonest, and the like. It also need not be something which is forced upon immigrants by unremitting hostility on the part of the locals (i. e. by racial prejudice). There may be sensible reasons for clustering together (they have already been listed on the previous page). It is even possible that contacts with fellow countrymen could facilitate adjustment to the local society rather than hinder it, especially if adjustment is understood to cover not only external aspects such as speaking the local language or wearing local clothes, but also internal aspects such as feeling that one has a place in the society.

Basically there seem to be two sets of factors encouraging

outsiders to form ethnic communities. One set encompasses pressures from without, which push the immigrants together as a kind of protective huddling reaction. These pressures include rejection, prejudice and discrimination. The other set involves the internal factors which draw the members of a minority group together. These include feelings of alienation from the majority society. At a more concrete level are opportunities to speak the mother tongue, the chance of getting advice from fellow countrymen, and the possibility of financial aid or other forms of assistance from kin. Ethnic neighbourhoods may act as a kind of "buffer mechanism" (Brody, 1970, p. 18) which helps immigrants to escape some of the strains of being a stranger in a strange land. Studies in, for example Australia (see Kovacs and Cropley, 1975, p. 32), have shown that contact with other immigrants of similar ethnic background reduces mental health failure in immigrants. Looking at the matter from the point of view of receiving societies, which are normally eager to avoid the formation of ghettoes (in the negative sense of the term), the crucial factor seems to be that of whether the immigrants cluster together because they are rejected by the receiving society, and therefore huddle as a defensive measure, or whether they are drawn together by the network of sentiment relations which has already been mentioned. In this latter case, provided that the necessary linking points with the majority society are available (jobs, social contacts, etc.), ethnic communities need not be regarded as an unmitigated disaster — indeed, they may even have a potential positive influence.

Dual alienation — people between two worlds

An important aspect of the position of immigrants to Great Britain has been strikingly stated by Khan (1977). They depend upon the United Kingdom for economic advancement, and must obtain entry to the local occupational/vocational system if they are to achieve this advancement. This requires a certain degree of adjustment to British ways. However, they are rejected by the locals, and they themselves reject certain aspects of life in Britain, with the result that they do not become fully assimilated to British life. To put it in another way, they remain at least partly estranged or alienated from the British society. At the same time, however, since some adjustment to British life is absolutely essential, a degree of estrangement from the ways of the mother country also occurs — it would normally be impossible, or at least very difficult, to adopt British norms while retaining those of the homeland absolutely unchanged. The result is that the immigrants are partly alienated from both societies.

Most immigrants depend upon the norms of the homeland for achieving status in their own community and, to some extent at least, govern their behaviour in Britain according to these norms. The norms of Britain are, however, decisive in day-to-day economic life. Immigrants thus depend upon both systems of norms (those of Britain and those of the homeland), but are full members of neither system. The situation is made even more acute by the fact that they cannot fully endorse or display the standards of either society, because to do so would have negative consequences in the other. In other words, they experience a state of dual alienation. As Foner (1977, p. 120) put it in describing the situation of immigrants from the West Indies, and Khan (1977, p. 81) in discussing Pakistanis, they are people whose lives are influenced by "two worlds", but they are full members of neither.

Indeed, the situation is probably even more complex than this. Life in the homeland is itself subject to processes of change, of which immigrants in Britain will be only partly aware. In addition, after a certain period of time and associated adjustment to life in Britain, immigrant communities develop local versions of their original lifeways. This means that immigrants are not only caught between two worlds but, in fact, that they fall between *three* worlds (Khan, 1977, p. 86): an idealized vision of the homeland, the reality of the local immigrant community, and the norms of the majority British society.

Dual assimilation

In earlier writings (e. g. Kovacs and Cropley, 1975) it has been argued that assimilation to a new society necessarily and inevitably requires estrangement from the earlier one. However, Putniņš (1976) and Smolicz and Secombe (1977) have both challenged this view, although writing from somewhat different standpoints. These authors argue that various patterns of assimilation which do not require giving up the ways of one society in order to acquire those of another are possible. Khan (1977) has specifically discussed this possibility in the context of immigrants to the United Kingdom. He pointed out that people between two worlds are not necessarily in a simple either/or situation, in which they must belong either to one world or to the other. Some immigrants in Britain seem to be able to "juggle two sets of values" (p. 83). One way of doing this is to take the norms necessary for economic advancement from the United Kingdom, those from which status and identity are derived from the homeland. However, people who achieve this juggling of values may pay a penalty in that they may never become fully fledged members of either society, although they need contacts with both to keep their identities intact.

Both Khan (1977) and Ballard and Ballard (1977) have suggested that a form of dual assimilation involving people able to function in two worlds while retaining an intact personality is emerging. Jeffcoate (1979) has also made a similar observation: he concluded that the self-image of Muslims in Britain has improved markedly in recent years, as they display greater determination to achieve their goals and increased pride in themselves. However, he pointed out that many British people see this emerging "black pride" (p. 22) as a bad thing, fearing that it means rejection of the British society, and indeed, a kind of reverse prejudice. Certainly, there are grounds for believing that this phenomenon of prejudice against the British actually does occur.

Consequences of alienation

One widely reported phenomenon in the relevant international literature is an increased incidence of what Power (1979, p. 116) called "culture related disorders" among immigrants. Kovacs and Cropley (1975) have reviewed studies covering a number of countries including the USA, Canada, Australia, Israel and Holland which reach a similar conclusion. In the case of Britain a number of studies suggest that it is true that, under certain circumstances, there are higher levels of psychiatric symptoms in immigrants in this country. Nicol (1974) referred to an early study which reported a higher level of affective disturbances among West Indian women than among British women. Bagley (1975) also cited earlier studies dealing with mental illness among immigrants in Britain. These studies suggested that rates of mental illness in both West Indians and Pakistanis are sometimes higher than among native Britons. Relatively common disorders among immigrants which have been mentioned by various authors include depression, paranoia, and schizophrenia.

Various writers have advanced differing explanations for the more frequent occurrence of mental illness in immigrants. Some theories argue that the phenomenon results from the fact that there is a higher tendency for unstable individuals to become immigrants in the first place — this is the "self-selection" theory reviewed by Sanua (1970). However, in view of the positive value attached to immigration in the social order in Pakistan and the West Indies, it seems unlikely that the self-selection theory is adequate for these countries. Other writers stress the importance of events in the receiving society, emphasizing, for instance, immigrants' lack of familiarity with "cues" (Hammet, 1965, p. 21) or "norms" (Tyehurst, 1951). Whereas, in the homeland, the immigrants could understand easily and effortlessly what was going on around them, in the receiving society they lack "cultural know how" (Hammet, 1965, p. 21). The result is a state of isolation or marginality or, as Tyehurst (p. 567) called it, "psychological rootlessness".

A second approach, discussed by David (1970), lays great emphasis upon the importance of the self-concept. In a new society immigrants are flooded with information which does not make sense to them, or which even contains contradictory messages. As a result, they experience considerable internal conflict, which results in a crisis of identity. A third, related approach is that of Eisenstadt (1954) who emphasized social roles. According to this analysis immigration involves disorganization of the system of learned roles in the old society. A simple example would be that of a former independent farmer who, after emigrating, found himself a faceless underling in a factory.

Bagley (1975) has applied this kind of analysis directly to West Indian immigrants in the United Kingdom. He interprets increased levels of mental illness among immigrants as resulting from the effect of a discrepancy between the aspirations which the immigrants possess, and the achievements which they actually manage. The British society teaches them that they should strive for certain kinds of goals and seek to become people of a certain kind (e. g. independent, skilled, able to make their own way in the world, able to earn their own keep, and so on), but denies them access to the means for achieving these goals (e. g. a good education, access to good jobs, promotion to higher positions, acceptance as members of social ingroups, and the like). This means that they learn simultaneously to strive for certain goals, but to be aware of the fact that they will never reach the goals — they experience a "double bind" (Bagley, 1975, p. 70).

The double bind places people in a problem situation where it is impossible for them to find a way out which both preserves self respect and, at the same time, leads to successful adaptation to the majority society. Pratt (1980) described mugging as seeming to offer a perfect way out for young West Indians in London: according to his analysis, the young men experience discrimination, most noticably in housing and education, develop feelings of frustration and resentment against the majority white society, and give vent to these by carrying our petty robberies with violence or the threat of violence, almost always against white victims. However, Pratt points out that the financial gains achieved in this way are so small as to lead to the conclusion that the real purpose of the muggings is not financial at all, but is to obtain revenge and achieve a feeling of being a worthwhile person. However, since such activities lead to increased public prejudice against West Indians in general, as well as causing clashes with the police when muggers are apprehended, their total effect is to exacerbate the problem they are supposed to solve (rejection by the majority society, discrimination, diminished sense of worth, etc.).

Closing remarks

The basic line of argument of the present chapter can be summarized fairly succinctly. As a result of being kept at arm's length by the British, while themselves rejecting certain aspects of British life but at the same time abandoning some of the norms of the motherland, immigrants experience only partial assimilation to the ways of Britain, and simultaneous partial estrangement from the ways of their homelands. This means that they are fully fledged members of neither society, but fall between two worlds. The psychological consequences of this state of affairs include bewilderment about their own identity, disappointment in the receiving society and in themselves, and feelings of hostility. The behavioural consequences include, in some cases, withdrawal from contact with the British society, in others aggressive or even criminal behaviour, and sometimes mental illness. The extreme negative manifestations which have just been mentioned — crime, mental illness, etc. — occur in only a small minority of cases. Nonetheless, the thesis of the present book is that the internal states of identity confusion, self-disappointment and the like are seen, to some extent at least, in nearly all immigrants.

In the following chapter the analysis of the situation of immigrants in terms of alienation, and especially dual alienation, or the state of being between two worlds, will be applied to immigrant children. Ultimately, after a review of existing approaches in Chapter 7, the implications of the present analysis for the education of immigrant children will be discussed in Chapter 8.

6

Immigrant Children: Children of Two Worlds

Special difficulties of children born in Britain

Immigrant children are, of course, the children of immigrants. However, as was mentioned in Chapter 2, there are at least three kinds of such children: those who were born in the motherland and spent some time as pupils there, those who were born in the motherland but came to the receiving society before starting school, and those who were born in the receiving society. Children born in the receiving society are frequently referred to as the "second generation", those who come to the receiving society at an early age as the "half second generation". Typically, it is assumed that the children who left the mother country at a relatively advanced age, such as 12, will be dominated in their psychological development by the socialization patterns of the mother country. The children who move to the receiving society at preschool age are thought likely to display a mixed pattern of socialization. Finally, it is frequently assumed that psychological development of the children actually born in the receiving society will be dominated by socialization into the ways of that society. This distinction suggests that the children who are actually born in the receiving society are likely to make the most rapid and most perfect adjustment to it, or, indeed, are likely to develop into "normal" citizens with only loose links to the mother country. This in turn seems to imply that adjustment problems will be at a minimum in these children.

Unfortunately, the evidence is that if anything this group experiences more difficulties of the kind outlined in Chapter 2.

On balance, the group which experiences the least difficulties is the one consisting of children who left the mother country at a relatively advanced age. In discussing evidence showing the greater difficulties of adjustment experienced by children born in the receiving society, Kovacs and Cropley (1975) hypothesized that this reflects the fact that these children have no firsthand experience with the ways of the mother country but are, nonetheless, expected by parents and other fellow countrymen to show familiarity with its norms. Paulston (1978) reported evidence on the adjustment of Finnish immigrants to Sweden which shows that differences between the three groups of children are not confined to fitting in with the standards and norms of the receiving society, but also involve acquisition of the new language. She found that children who moved to Sweden at the age of 12 eventually achieved language skills comparable to those of native-born Swedish children, although the process of acquisition of the Swedish language was slower for them than for Swedish children. Children who moved to Sweden at preschool age or were born there experienced difficulties in learning Swedish, and often failed to master the language at all. Worst off were the children who had started school in Finland just before emigrating to Sweden.

In the case of West Indian and Pakistani immigrants in Britain, it seems to be true that there is a special problem involving the youngsters who were actually born in this country. For many of them the norms of the United Kingdom are the only norms with which they have any firsthand experience, and they know the mother country only through what their parents tell them, what they learn via books or the mass media, and from other indirect sources. On experiencing rejection or discrimination, they do not even have the consolation of looking back on the advantages of the mother country or of being able to look forward to the time when they can go home, since for all practical purposes they are already home. When these children experience rejection or discrimination, the alienating effect may be particularly difficult to cope with (Foner, 1977; Bagley, 1979). For example Bagley, Mallick and

Verma (1979) found that West Indian girls born in Britain had lower levels of self-esteem than those born in the West Indies. As a result, children born here may react with particularly high levels of resentment and anger, showing hostility to authority figures, particularly the police, as well as truculence and aggression at school. They may, for instance, refuse to take available low status jobs, because they do not see why they should tolerate shabby treatment (Jeffcoate, 1979). A paradox for children born in Britain is thus that they may be more open to the acceptance of British norms, but that this may lead to less satisfaction with life in this country.

Immigrants born outside Britain (especially Asians) sometimes seek to avoid being "contaminated" (Khan, 1977, p. 74) by British life, but those born here are much less likely to try to avoid learning British life ways. This difference between immigrants born in Britain and those born elsewhere can be understood by comparing the role of the homeland for the two groups (Ballard and Ballard, 1977). In the case of immigrants whose major socialization experiences were in the mother country, the homeland provides the mother tongue, the religious orientation, kinship attitudes (traditional friends and foes), and standards for judging or achieving status, as well as guidance on many practical matters such as food preferences. It thus provides the norms for guiding much of ordinary day-to-day behaviour. By contrast, in the case of persons born in the United Kingdom the homeland provides merely a cultural heritage. In other words, for these people the homeland provides a broad framework rather than detailed guidelines for the conduct of everyday life.

As Mullard (1973) summarized the situation: immigrant children born in the United Kingdom are personally acquainted only with British norms, but are expected to show due regard for the ways of the mother country. They are also simultaneously attracted to an idealized image of life in the homeland as well as to the way of life in Britain. However, British norms include rejection of the homeland, so that both sets of norms cannot be endorsed at the same time. Finally, the children are kept at arm's length by the British, and are refused admission to full membership of British society, despite the fact that many of them "feel" British. This raises particular problems of identity development. The children must ask themselves (Verma and Mallick, 1978, p. 7): "Am I British or not?" Their accent may say "Yes", but their skin colour may say "No". Finally, these children may believe that they have a perfect right to be in Britain because they were born here. As a result they may be less able to find ways of reconciling themselves to discrimination or inferior status, and thus less able to resolve the identity conflicts just outlined.

Prejudice among children

Despite the differences among various groups of immigrant children just described, the balance of the present chapter, and indeed of the present book, will speak of "immigrant children" and will offer various generalizations which refer to such children as though they comprise a single homogeneous group. This should not be taken as indicating a belief that factors such as the age of coming to Britain are unimportant, but as reflecting a desire to develop a broad approach capable of serving as the basis for more specific considerations of particular groups of immigrant children or, indeed, of individual children.

As was the case with adults, immigrant children experience a considerable degree of hostility and rejection by British children — their school mates. Bagley and Verma (1975, p. 258) refer to "a depressing amount of hostility" and "a disturbing reservoir of hostility". This was more virulent in the case of Pakistanis than West Indians, a finding which Bagley and Verma attributed to the more distinct dress, religion and other customs of Pakistanis — they are more "visible". In studies with 14—16 years olds, these authors reported that about 70 per cent of the comments made about immigrants in free descriptions written by the children were negative.

In summarizing the literature in the area of children's racial attitudes in Britain, Jeffcoate (1979) concluded that children are aware of racial attitudes by the age of three, can elucidate stereotypical social and economic roles for immigrants by the age of five, and that by 11 or 12 British children are thoroughly familiar with the society's prejudices and stereotypes. In a study of prejudice in young children in the UK, he showed how negative attitudes to immigrants remained relatively hidden when teachers controlled the children's responses, but emerged when the children were encouraged to respond freely. In discussions of pictures and in stories made up by children about favoured and non-favoured lands, two broad negative stereotypes of countries such as Pakistan and the West Indies emerged. The first of these was the "Oxfam image" according to which these countries, along with other non-European countries, are dominated by poverty, starvation and disease. The second negative stereotype was the "Tarzan image", according to which the people in those countries paint their faces, swing from trees, eat raw meat, and so on. Thus, immigrant children are the object of considerable prejudice on the part of their British classmates.

The immigrants are aware of at least some of this prejudice. Jeffcoate found that 10- and 11-year-old Pakistanis complained that they did not like being called racial names such as "Wog" or "Black Sambo". When 9- to 11-year-old Pakistani children told stories, a number of them told of wanting to go "home". Jeffcoate (1979, p. 17) concluded that this reflected, not a love of Pakistan, but a reaction to the "sense of being rejected". Kovacs and Cropley (1975) extended this line of argument by emphasizing the importance in such behaviour of "exaggerated ethnicity". This phenomenon involves a tendency to regard the original homeland as the embodiment of all that is good. It may go so far as to include refusal to use the language of the receiving society, even after this language has been learned. It is thus a form of chauvinism, although one which is often regarded as admirable. In Britain, Ballard and Ballard (1977) detected exaggerated ethnicity in second generation Sikhs with whom they worked. Jeffcoate (1979) also reported that some Pakistani children reacted to being called names by proclaiming that they were proud of being brown, and jeering at the behaviour of the white children on the grounds that it reflected jealousy. Jeffcoate also gave examples of West Indian children's romantic view of the West Indies as a land of beauty, music, endless leisure and untold plenty.

When the phenomenon develops to the point that it impairs realistic relationships with the British society, exaggerated ethnicity can have effects similar to those seen in racism. It can lead to dealing with members of the white community in terms of negative stereotypes, deliberately remaining aloof from British life ways, and assuming that anything bad which happens is a result of ill will on the part of the British. Such reactions have the potential to be as destructive as white racism directed against coloured immigrants. As a result, it is hard to agree with those writers who have praised conscious and deliberate rejection of the British society by coloured immigrants. Although it is clear that refusing to accept jobs on the grounds that to do so would be to capitulate to a racist white society could be regarded as an act of self-assertion, and therefore as preferable to passive acceptance of prejudice, it is difficult to see how such an approach offers any prospects for long term healthy adjustment. The danger also exists that this kind of reaction can become a mere alibi.

Children between two worlds

For the purpose of the present discussion, the crucial problem for immigrant children is that they are simultaneously exposed to two sets of norms — those of the homeland and those of the receiving society. This is, of course, also the problem of adult immigrants, but in the case of children it takes on a special form, since it is during childhood that the process of identity development is at its most intensive. Identity development itself is never free of conflict. Achieving the transition from being a baby under the care of protective parents to that of being an independent person who can work within the constraints of a particular society (i. e. who has been socialized) is a relatively difficult process for all children. The process of growing up is, in fact, accompanied by "normal" problems of what Keniston (1965, p. 456) called "developmental estrangement".

Immigrant children, however, experience this process under particularly difficult circumstances. This is because one set of socializing influences ("primary" in nature — parents, family members, etc.) attempts to pass on to the children the norms of the motherland, while another set of socializing influences ("secondary" in nature — school, local children, sports heroes, mass media, etc.) transmits the norms of the receiving society. The local children are also exposed to these two broad sets of socializing influences, but in their case there is a high level of agreement between the norms espoused by the family and those endorsed by sources of socialization outside the family. In the case of immigrant children, however, there may be considerable disagreement or even clear conflict between socializing forces in the home and those in the community. This disagreement may include remarkably different notions concerning concrete matters like dress and food habits, and also differences in values, morals, aspirations, and the like. In Britain this is true both for West Indian children (Foner, 1977) and also for Asians (Ballard and Ballard, 1977).

As Zubrzycki (1964, p. 117) put it, immigrant children are "familiar with two sets of frequently conflicting behaviour standards simultaneously and from competing authoritative sources". The point was made in a slightly different way by Hansen (1940, p. 93) who, writing of Norwegian immigrant children in the United States, pointed out that: "The Norwegian father considered his children Norwegians; the children considered themselves Americans. In reality they were neither". Other writers have used different metaphors to describe the situation. Harris (1962, p. 61) described immigrant children as being "in a vacuum between two cultures", Listwan (1960, p. 42) as being "thrown between two patterns of culture" and Jupp (1966, p. 74) as "torn between two cultures".

It would be possible to give many specific British examples of this phenomenon of disagreement between local norms and those of the mother countries of West Indian and Pakistani immigrant children. Ballard and Ballard (1977) have summarized the situation as it applies to Asian children, pointing out that their homes are likely to stress loyalty to the family, respect for elders, fulfilment of obligations, hard work, and obedience to parents. The British society, on the other hand, stresses individualism, freedom, self-satisfaction, breaking away from the influence of parents, and similar ideals. In discussing the situation of immigrant children in Britain and the fact that they must try to adjust simultaneously to two competing sets of norms, several writers, including Foner (1977) and Khan (1977) have described them as being "between two worlds", a metaphor which neatly summarizes the line of argument developed to date in the present book.

Conflict with parents

One of the results for immigrant children of being exposed to socializing influences outside the home which compete with the admonitions of their parents is that they are "pulled away for their parents" (Taylor, 1976, p. 9). The result is a "gulf of intergenerational conflict" (p. 9). Such conflict is by no means confined to the United Kingdom, but is a more or less universal phenomenon in immigrant families (see Kovacs and Cropley, 1975 and Cropley, 1982 for discussions of the phenomenon of conflict with parents in Australia and the Federal Republic of Germany).

One area of parent-child conflict identified by Foner (1977) results from incongruities between parents' levels of aspiration and those of the children. There are also conflicts over religious or moral behaviour, with parents not infrequently expecting their children to accept a religion which is regarded by the majority society as odd or as involving strange customs (such as the wearing of the turban by Sikhs). In Britain, as in many other immigrant receiving countries, a common source of conflict with parents centers on differences between the norms of the mother country and those of the British society concerning the amount of freedom to be allowed to adolescent girls. For example many Pakistani parents do not regard obtaining an advanced education as a high priority goal for girls (Khan, 1977). According to the traditional norms, more important goals for girls are the maintenance of an unblemished reputation and the learning of correct manners, in the hope of eventually contracting a "good" marriage. In Britain, by contrast, schools and other socializing agencies tend to teach girls to become more independent and to strive for a high degree of self-development. In the eyes of immigrant parents, girls are often led astray by schoolmates, fashion magazines, the cinema and contacts with boys. According to John (1971, p. 31) many immigrant adolescents complain that their parents cling to old fashioned values. Ironically, the youngsters see these values as those of Victorian England! Perhaps the crucial point at which the conflict between parents and children comes to a head is reached when the children make plans to marry. If the parents cannot control the choice of mate for their children there is a serious danger that the "chain of culture" will be broken (Taylor, 1976, p. 133). In the case of Asian young people, there are grounds for believing that, at least until recently, the wishes of the parents were prevailing in considerably more than half of all cases (e. g. Taylor, 1976; Ballard and Ballard, 1977).

It is worth repeating again at this point that conflict between children and their parents, especially during adolescence, is by no means confined to immigrants: the "generation gap" has become a cliché in discussing relations between parents and their children. However, as with other developmental problems, immigrant children experience the usual difficulties associated with the process of growing up in a form exacerbated by the fact that, in addition to being children, they are immigrants. Furthermore, the complaint of immigrant children that their parents are out of date may have more truth than in the case of the generation gap between British children and their parents. In the latter case, it is true that the parents acquired their own norms in the British society as it existed 20 or 30 years ago, but at least the parents have had the opportunity in the meantime of living in the local society and adapting to it as it has changed around them. Immigrant parents, on the other hand, may have been isolated from the mother country for a number of years. As a result, they may be unaware of changes which have occurred in the norms which they wish to transmit to their children. They may, in fact, be trying to develop in their children a set of norms which no longer exist, even in the homeland.

Khan (1977) has discussed this problem with particular reference to Pakistani immigrants in the United Kingdom. Former Pakistani villagers now living in this country may be unaware of recent changes in the homeland. These include changes in family life resulting from rapid industrialization, increasing availability of education for girls, greater tolerance of social contacts between boys and girls, and erosion of the old system of arranged marriages. This means that the parents may themselves be alienated from the present norms of the homeland, and may be trying to adjust their children to a world which no longer exists.

The double bind

A special problem involving the exposure of immigrant children to two competing sources of socializing experiences is the problem of education. According to Dove (1975) no fewer than 90 per cent of Asian and 80 per cent of West Indian 15—16 year olds in London reported that they wished to obtain at least the 0-Level. Taylor (1976) has also reported that many Pakistani students are keen to continue even beyond 0-Levels. Immigrant parents also recognize that obtaining an education is crucial for the advancement of their children in the United Kingdom (Khan, 1977). The position of immigrants, then, is that education is highly valued and is correctly identified as being essential for achieving success in Britain. At the same time, however, the school is probably the single most powerful agent threatening maintenance of the norms of the homeland. Schools reflect the values of the dominant society, which include among other things, prejudice against immigrants. Thus, immigrant parents who encourage their children to succeed in school are also encouraging the children to accept norms which conflict with those of the mother country, and may even be encouraging their children to be prejudiced against their own parents. This means that success in British schools is desirable, but also threatening (unless, of course, the alienating effect ceases to exist).

The situation may thus be described as involving a "double bind". The more immigrant parents encourage their children to accept the norms of British schools, the more they also encourage alienation from the ways of the mother country, and even from themselves. The children too experience a state of affairs in which they simultaneously accept and reject the ways of the homeland and of Britain, or of their own parents. Brah (1973) gives a good example of this ambivalence in the case of young Asians. They simultaneously disliked their parents' "interference" in their lives, but valued highly the feelings of warmth and security generated by it. Not only individuals but also institutions are affected by the double bind phenomenon: the more schools seek to make themselves interesting and attractive to immigrant children by adjusting their curriculum in ways which support and maintain the norms of Pakistan or the West Indies, the more they risk offering a programme which will hinder adjustment to the real world of life in Britain. This whole issue will be discussed more fully in Chapters 7 and 8.

Alienation from Britain

Immigrant children are children between two worlds. They are constantly exposed to the norms of the British society and, to a considerable degree, accept the norms. However, they are frequently rejected or at least kept at arm's length by the majority of British society. They may even be placed in the double bind position according to which increasing acceptance of British norms means increasing rejection of the norms of the homeland and, therefore, indirectly of their parents and of themselves. They are also exposed, primarily through their parents, to the norms of the homeland, and are often strongly attracted to the image of life there which is presented by the parents. This image is, not infrequently, unrealistically idealized. There may also be irreconcilable clashes between the two systems of norms, so that moving towards more total acceptance of one set cannot be achieved without moving away from the other. Where the children's rate of adjustment to the British society is more rapid than that of the parents (the normal state of affairs), the conflict between the norms of the two worlds may make itself visible in clashes between children and parents.

The imperfect adjustment of immigrant children to life between two worlds also leads to clashes with the receiving society, a problem which appears to be more acute for West Indian than for Pakistani youngsters. This reflects, among other factors, the belief of West Indians that they are native speakers of the English language, whereas they may find that the British cannot understand the things they say. It also seems to be true that the desire of West Indian immigrants to achieve integration into the British society is much stronger than that of Pakistanis. Consequently rejection by the British is more difficult for the West Indians to handle. It should also be mentioned that West Indians come from a society where there is considerable prejudice against Blacks. Thus, it might be anticipated that West Indian immigrants would be much more vulnerable to rejection of their own blackness than would Pakistanis, since many West Indians would actually share with the British prejudice against Blacks. The greater feeling of self-doubt and insecurity because of their skin colour would be expected to lead to extremely strong emotional reactions in West Indians. This speculation is consistent with the recent emergence of a particularly militant exaggerated ethnicity in some West Indian immigrants. Other factors, such as the much more close-knit family structure among Pakistanis and the greater emphasis on obedience to parents would also be expected to help to cushion young Pakistanis from the psychological effects of rejection by the members of the British society.

Research in at least two areas of maladjustment to life in Britain is generally consistent with the expectation that West Indians would have the greatest difficulty in coping with prejudice and discrimination. About 10 years ago McGlashan (1972) commented on the higher than average involvement of West Indian adolescents in petty crimes of violence in the streets ("mugging"). This topic is a particularly sensitive one, as many West Indian spokesmen draw attention to the disproportionately high number of young West Indians who are questioned by the police as suspects, and argue that the frequency of involvement of their young countrymen in muggings is much less than the public believes is the case. Nonetheless, it is certainly true that the popular stereotype of West Indians, especially in London, is that they are much more frequently involved in delinquency than are British teenagers. This opinion seems to be supported by available statistics: Pratt (1980) studied a random sample of 1,000 muggings in London, and showed that although 90 per cent of the victims were white, 60 per cent of the muggers were black. Despite this, it should be borne in mind that only a small percentage of black youths carries out the muggings in question — most young West Indians are not muggers!

By contrast, studies such as those by Lambert (1970) and Taylor (1976) found that there was a very low level of delinquency among Pakistani immigrants in Birmingham and Newcastle. Indeed, Taylor's adolescent Pakistanis criticized British lads for their rebelliousness and destructiveness. Taylor concluded that the low involvement of Pakistani youngsters in delinquency was directly attributable to their traditions of orderly social behaviour and obedience to parents. Generally, the lack of clarity about the involvement of immigrants in Britain in juvenile delinquency is consistent with the literature on the subject in other countries. As Kovacs and Cropley (1975) showed, there is a tendency for members of receiving societies to believe that immigrants are disproportionately frequently involved in delinquent behaviour. Furthermore, some immigrant children do engage in such behaviour, those born in the receiving society more frequently than local children. However, delinquency is by no means universal among immigrant children. On the contrary, it is engaged in by only a small percentage. The situation seems to be very similar in the United Kingdom.

Personal problems of immigrant children have already been mentioned in Chapter 2. It was reported there that, for example, the incidence of "behaviourally deviant" West Indian boys and girls was between two and three times as high as for British children. It was also reported that West Indian pupils are often described as aggressive, destructive, hostile and abusive or, in the case of girls, solitary, miserable and fearful. Bagley (1972) referred to the increased incidence of "behaviour disorder" and "emotional disturbance" in immigrant children, while Bagley, Mallick and Verma (1979) reported increased neuroticism and lower self-esteem in these children. Jeffcoate (1979, p. 12) concluded that by the age of 11 or 12 they already show "ambivalence", "self-denial", "identity conflict" and "personality disorder". Interestingly, these are precisely the kinds of disturbed behaviours which have been observed among immigrant pupils in the Federal Republic of Germany (Akpinar, Bendit, Lopez-Blasco and Zimmer, 1978). This suggests that there is a disruption of immigrant children's ability to deal effectively with the external world, which is not confined to West Indians in Britain.

The role of socioeconomic status

Many immigrant children are of relatively low socioeconomic status. This is true not only of Pakistanis and West Indians in the United Kingdom, but of immigrant children throughout Western Europe (Steedman, 1979). Not only is low socioeconomic status frequently associated with factors such as negative attitudes to language as a tool for dealing with the world and a preference for actions rather than talk, lower skill in manipulating abstract concepts, negative attitudes to school, unfavourable self-image in relationship to school, and similar factors, but it frequently means that the children in question experience pronounced physical disadvantages which militate against their achieving high status in the community.

For example, studies of immigrant families such as the work of Rutter, Yule, Morton and Bagley (1975) have shown that a higher percentage of immigrant children have parents who are unskilled or semiskilled workers, that they more frequently come from families with a significantly higher proportion of working mothers, and that they come from much larger families than average. Associated with these phenomena, or resulting from them, are disadvantages such as overcrowding. Rutter and his colleagues showed that 40 per cent of the immigrant children in their study lived in houses where amenities such as kitchen or bathroom or lavatory had to be shared, and that 40 per cent lived in multiple-occupancy dwellings. Among native born children, by contrast, the figures were 20 per cent or less in both cases. As a result, the children have little or no access to books and little privacy or quiet for activities such as doing homework. They may also have to help with housework or with the supervision of younger brothers and sisters and may, in any case, place little value on middle class activities such as going to school, since it may not seem to them to be something which is valuable for getting along in life.

Although it is clear that many immigrant children share certain disadvantages with local children of low socioeconomic status, many of the studies already cited in this book have shown that they are frequently further below average than can be explained merely on the basis of socioeconomic status. Thus, this does not seem to be a satisfactory explanation on its own. Other contributing factors in Britain which are strongly associated with being an immigrant include lack of familiarity with local forms of the English language, as well as rejection and discrimination on the part of the locals. Bagley and Verma (179) have also drawn attention to the problem of racial prejudice; this may even include prejudice on the part of teachers (Bagley, 1975a; Jeffcoate, 1979). In the case of immigrant children, then, they seem to experience not only the "normal" problems associated with low socioeconomic status, but additional problems which are connected with the fact that they are immigrants. As Townsend and Brittan (1972) put it, immigrant children experience special problems to do with culture and language which are added on to the usual problems and difficulties experienced by all children.

In Chapter 2 a number of studies were cited showing that the achievement of immigrant pupils in British schools is often inferior to that of British children. Nonetheless, it was pointed out that some studies have not confirmed this — a recent report by Driver (1980), for example, showed that among over 2000 school leavers in five multiracial schools the highest average marks were obtained by West Indian girls. A study by Bagley, Bart and Wong (1978) which integrated data on achievement and personal psychological adjustment helps clarify the dynamics of achievement in immigrant pupils. They divided West Indian pupils in London into three groups on the basis of a combination of school, home and self-image variables, and compared the groups' achievement in school. Two of the groups did badly, but the third did well: it consisted not of low, but of high, achievers. Bagley and his colleagues then showed that there were certain common characteristics shared by the children who had done well in school. They came from homes with good material circumstances, had positive expectations of school and work, and possessed favourable self-images. They were well adjusted to the British society, and also to their own ethnic identity. By contrast, the two groups of low achieving children came from homes marked by poor material circumstances, low expectations of self and school, and poor self-image. These data are particularly interesting in the present context, since they suggest that immigrant children can do well in British schools when they succeed in adapting themselves to British norms without loss of self-esteem — in other words when they succeed in adjusting themselves to both worlds.

Self-alienation

The thesis of the present book is that by being thrown between two worlds immigrant children are placed in a double-bind position where they are, so to speak, neither fish nor fowl. The more "British" they become, the less they accept those aspects of themselves which are clearly not British. In other words, adjustment to the British norms requires them to reject their own "foreign" characteristics, or to become alienated from themsleves. This is the phenomenon which Coard and Coard (1971) called "self-contempt" or "rejection of ethnic identity", while Weinreich (1979a) called it "self-rejection". This self-alienation is essentially a problem of identity conflict. Especially helpful as an aid to understanding in this context is the distinction between "cultural identity" and "personal identity" (Weinreich, 1979b): cultural identity involves acceptance of the norms of a particular society, personal identity, on the other hand, derives from a sense of belonging to a particular group. If the process of adoption of the values, habits, attitudes, and the like, of the receiving society is not accompanied by a feeling of belonging as an individual person to some respected group, the result is self-alienation. Even more difficult is the situation in which the norms of the receiving society actually conflict with those factors which lead to this feeling of belonging; i. e. when development of a cultural identity damages the individual identity. As will become apparent from the examples which follow, even immigrants who have achieved a good adaptation in the sense of cultural identity may experience enormous difficulties in the area of personal identity. The resulting identity conflict leads, not infrequently, according to Verma and Mallick (1978, p. 5) to development of "a sense of masked inferiority". For example, West Indian pupils may describe themselves as speaking "bad" English or as coming from a "bad" family (Jeffcoate, 1979, p. 76).

Mullard (1973, p. 14) has dramatized this uncertainty or even rejection of their own identity in immigrant children by referring to being "a little white boy in a black skin". Jeffcoate gave the example (p. 22) of a four-year-old who denied that he was black and insisted that he was white. He also gave the example (p. 23) of a black girl, Deputy Head Girl in her school, who was heard to remark "you can't trust coloureds". In achieving a certain degree of success in the dominant white system, the girl had picked up, and was willing to express verbally, prejudice against other Blacks. Ironically, however, she was not totally accepted by the white children in the school, so that her position was very much that of being between two worlds, a full member of neither.

This alienation from their own racial group among immigrant children has been demonstrated very strikingly by Milner (1975). Asian and West Indian youngsters of five to eight years of age were shown dolls or pictures of children of their own racial group and also of white children. They were asked to say which doll or picture was most like them. No fewer than 48 per cent of the West Indians identified the white doll as being most like them, while 24 per cent of Asian children also described the white doll as being most like them. In commenting on the doll or picture which actually represented their own racial group, 58 per cent of West Indian children and 45 per cent of the Asians said that this doll was "bad" and 82 per cent and 77 per cent respectively said that it was "ugly". This study shows in a striking way the devaluation of their own racial group among immigrant children. It is this phenomenon which is referred to here as "self-alienation".

The problem of being between two worlds and the associated danger of self-alienation, with the possible resulting emergence of delinquent behaviour, aggression, withdrawal or depression will be the key concept in discussions in the balance of this book concerning education and immigrant children in Britain. The basis of these discussions can be relatively succinctly stated. Immigrant children experience, in addition to the normal problems of growing up, the difficulty that they stand between two worlds. This leads, almost inevitably to disagreement and confusion, and frequently manifests itself in undesirable ways. These may range from conflicts with parents (which go beyond the normal conflicts experienced by most adolescents and their parents), to a sense of uncertainty or doubt, and occasionally to exaggerated ethnicity which can become so pronounced as to constitute inverse racism. Sometimes self-alienation manifests itself in delinquent or criminal behaviour, and sometimes in behaviour requiring psychiatric intervention. The task of the schools is seen as being that of minimizing the degree of conflict between worlds, and helping immigrant children to cope with the situation.

The role of language

An aspect of psychological development and of adjustment to the receiving society which is of such importance as to warrant separate discussion is the dual question of the role of the mother tongue in the adjustment of immigrant children, and that of how to teach them English or, in the case of West Indian children, how to promote the use of standard forms of English. It has already been pointed out in Chapter 3 that language is far more than a neutral communication instrument like a typewriter, but that it is a crucial element in the formation and maintenance of personality (e. g. Egger, 1977; Titone, 1978). For immigrant children, then, the mother tongue is a vital link with the norms of the homeland, and inadequate mastery of it represents a serious disruption of relationships with the original culture. It also represents a disruption of relationships with parents, not only because a shared language means shared norms, but, in some cases, for the simple reason that the parents may be unable to speak any other language. At the same time, mastery of standard English is crucial for success in British schools and for later success in the British society. The ideal situation for immigrant children would, of course, be mastery of both languages, in other words bilingualism. Unfortunately, as will be shown in Chapter 7, this state is not always achieved.

Suffice it to say here that many immigrant children experience difficulties arising from inadequate mastery of English. These can be understood, to some extent at least, in terms of alienation. The children are living in a society where the English language (for them a foreign language or at least a foreign dialect) holds undisputed sway, and where mastery of English has important consequences for their lives. Failure to master English delivers the children into the "language trap" (Honey, 1983): at school, for instance, it means that they are unable to follow instruction properly, are unable to express their thoughts clearly and accurately, and are likely to receive poor marks even in situations where they really possess the necessary knowledge. Their chances of experiencing success are reduced, with negative consequences for both motivation and belief in their own competence. This raises the possibility of a psychological reaction involving rejection of school, rejection of English and of British norms, feelings of hopelessness, a sense of despair or rage, and entanglement in a web of self-perpetuating difficulties.

On the other hand, an immigrant child who speaks perfect English has greatly enhanced prospects of becoming fully integrated into British society and of avoiding such problems. At the same time, however, Urdu, Pushtu, or Punjabi, as well as West Indian dialects of English, are regarded by many members of the majority British society as being the languages of despised outgroups. This means that mastering English raises a serious danger of abandoning or of at least being pulled away from the norms of the mother country. Indeed, fear on the part of immigrant parents that mastery of English will lead to rejection of the mother tongue is probably not without foundation. This means that, when considering how and in what way to support their children's acquisition of standard English, parents are once again faced with the double bind which has already been mentioned. The more they encourage the children to learn and use English, the more they promote their children's alienation from the motherland and indeed, from themselves. The more they discourage the use of English, the less the children's prospects of achieving status and economic advancement in Britain. What this problem means for practical classroom procedures will be dealt with at length later.

Closing remarks

A particular point of view of relationships between immigrants and the receiving society has been developed. This point of view has been applied to the "problem" of immigrant children — the problem that they fall "between two worlds". The final two chapters of the book now turn to the question of what this analysis means for schools. Chapter 7 contains an overview of the role of school, and Chapter 8 offers a number of criticisms and suggestions. In order to avoid establishing excessively high expectations in readers' minds, it is important to point out that the review, criticisms and suggestions are not presented in the form of detailed analyses of curriculum. What the final two chapters contain is an attempt to develop guidelines for good practice, so that schools can function in a more constructive way.

7
The Educational Response: Approaches to Date

A task for schools

Immigrant children experience various difficulties which have already been outlined. Many of these are the result of their exposure to competing sets of norms, those of the mother country on the one hand (in the present case Pakistan and the West Indies), those of the receiving society on the other (in the present case Britain). Although the home is in all probability the most important mediator of values, norms, beliefs and the like, next to the home the single most important socializing agency is the school (Cross, Happel, Doston and Stiles, 1976). Educators also have the advantage that they are usually conscious of their role as socializers, whereas parents frequently are not. Thus, it does not seem unreasonable to call upon schools to make a major contribution to "solving the problem" of immigrants, although as will be emphasized more fully later, schools cannot be expected to eliminate all difficulties alone. The purpose of the present chapter is to review the role of school in this respect, with particular emphasis on Britain.

The role of school in society

Stated succinctly, schools have the task of preparing children for life in the society in which they will live (e. g. Townsend and Brittan, 1973). This means that children should acquire in school an accurate picture of the "real" world (Jeffcoate, 1979). Nowadays, however, most writers go beyond the point of seeing school merely as a place for transmitting knowledge about the *status quo*. They emphasize that, in addition, schools have great potential for communicating to pupils an image of what the world *could* be like, or even what it *should* be like. Although the danger of reducing school to an instrument for the dispensing of propaganda must be borne in mind, even writers who stress this danger usually accept that, in addition to their "conservative" role, schools can contribute to "transforming" society (e. g. OECD, 1974; Goutman, 1977).

The conservative role involves transmitting the particular society's view of what is right, and legitimizing this view, for instance by emphasizing that it works, is time-hallowed, is self-evidently correct, stems from divine revelation, or follows the precepts of some sage whose wisdom cannot be questioned. The transforming role involves examining the origins of accepted givens, drawing attention to alternatives, evaluating the consequences of the *status quo* and of various alternative possibilities, in short, of reevaluating the cultural heritage of norms, values, standards, interpersonal relations, etc. As Townsend (1971) pointed out, the question of what values and norms schools should try to transmit is much more than simply a paedagogical one. It is also a socio-political question having much to do with the kind of society a nation's people wants or is led to believe it wants, as well as with the relative ability of different sectors of society with different visions of what it should be like to make their visions clear and "sell" them to the public, policy makers, or practitioners such as teachers. *Multicultural education* is an approach stressed by commentators who wish to avoid social fragmentation in Britain and hope to see one nation, albeit one which differs from what exists at present, emerge from the present mixture of "real" Britons and outsiders (e. g. Townsend and Brittan, 1973; Jeffcoate, 1979).

In addition to the distinction between school's conserving and transforming functions, a second dichotomy of considerable relevance to the discussion of school and immigrant children is the distinction between its *inter*personal as against its *intra*personal role. What is meant here is that schools have one set of functions primarily concerned with helping children get along with other people (interpersonal functions), and another set which has to do with development of each child's own self, especially fostering of a positive self-image (intrapersonal functions). Actually, the two aspects are part of the same whole. For example, a positive self-image helps in getting along with other people. However, for simplicity of discussion they will be distinguished from one another here. Hurrelmann (1979) has referred to the "key role" (p. 19) of school in these two aspects of development. This role includes:

(a) preparing children to fit into the existing structure of society;
(b) legitimizing this structure;
(c) developing each child's own capacities;
(d) fostering the emergence of an individual identity and a sense of self.

Major questions which will be discussed later in this chapter can be approached in terms of these various distinctions. Should schools seek to adapt children (particularly immigrant children) to the reality of present society, or should they seek to foster the emergence of a different kind of society? Should schools focus on helping immigrant children fit themselves into the existing social structure, or should they seek to achieve the maximum individual development of each child? Are these latter two goals necessarily contradictory (i. e. must fitting in in the British society involve sacrificing self-development)?

Dimensions of the school's response

For most immigrant children UK schools provide the first organized direct contact with British ways. As Khan (1977) has pointed out, this means not only a setting in which standard forms of the English language hold undisputed sway, but one in which most of the participants espouse values and accept norms which are, to some degree at least, new to the immigrant child, since both fellow pupils and teachers will usually be members of the majority society, with all the social-psychological implications of that state of affairs. (Of course there are schools in which immigrants are actually in the majority, so that in their case the statement just made will not be strictly true. Even here, however, the acknowledged "correct" language will be English, while the institutional values as reflected in lesson content, learning materials, even physical organization of the school, will be dominated by British customs.) These new norms include ideas about the rights and responsibilities of each individual which differ in certain respects from those of the children's homeland (or often, more accurately, those of their parents), and even more importantly, they may include negative attitudes towards immigrants in general, or even towards the immigrant child's own race. In other words, the first contact with school can involve a massive assault on the child's self-respect, or even identity.

An important feature of British schools is that, even today, failure to adjust to the presence of large numbers of immigrant children "... permeates almost every aspect of the school curriculum" (Townsend and Brittan, 1973, p. 7). As Saunders (1980, p. 32) put it:

"... in some schools there is a reluctance to recognize the increased heterogeneity of the pupil population; in many others, even when the fact is acknowledged, there is no agreement on the criteria that might be followed in developing or adopting relevant curricula; and in yet others curricular modifications are limited, for example, to the teaching of English as a second language and religious studies."

The schools tend, in a variety of ways, to "ignore", "underestimate" or even "disparage" the school potential of immigrants (Jeffcoate, 1979, p. 38). How subtly this can be done has been shown by Deslonde (1976) in a good description of an apparently successful multiracial classroom in action. Minority group children (Deslonde was writing about the USA) are playing with the teacher, using a toy house as the basis of their game, and the atmosphere seems to be one of racial acceptance and respect. However, the house is clearly that of a middle class white family, and the values and norms depicted are also those of such a family — hence they may bear little relationship to the lives of the minority group children. As a result the game makes clear to them that they are deviants or of inferior status. Even today, perceived shortcomings of this kind in British schools have led to actions such as the attempt by a group of Sikhs in Southall in December 1980 to buy a local school and convert it into a Sikh school.

The problem is partly a matter of content, with children learning, for instance, about Alfred the Great but ignoring the history of Asia or the West Indies, or about the Wars of the Roses but not the causes and consequences of recent immigration to this country. (Of course this is not to suggest that there is no place for the study of British history in British schools. Quite the contrary, as the schools have an important role in transmitting the national culture.) However, the whole issue goes beyond simply subject matter: as a matter of fact, as Saunders (1980) pointed out, since basic literacy, numeracy and social skills are just as important for immigrant children as for majority group children, a great deal of the content of school curriculum would be unaffected by the presence of minority group pupils in the classroom. Even more important than simply content are the methods and materials through which content is transmitted. These can, for instance, be full of misconceptions, preconceptions and unfavourable stereotypes (Weinberg, 1976; Jeffcoate, 1979), so that children are surrounded by "negative racial bias" (NUT, 1981). Quite apart from considerations such as accuracy or even fair play, disparaging immigrants can be expected to have serious negative effects on the self-image of immigrant children, on the attitudes of their British classmates, and even on those of teachers, with the various unfavourable consequences which have been spelled out in earlier chapters.

The whole matter goes even further, involving not only "objective" factors such as the contents of lessons or the choice of textbooks, but also the subjective factor constituted by the human participants, in particular teachers. To quote Deslonde (1976, p. 72), the teacher is "a vitally important link in any multicultural effort", a point of view endorsed, though in somewhat different contexts, by British writers such as Bagley (1975) and Jeffcoate (1979). Teachers, in addition to their role in what have just been called "objective" aspects of instruction, transmit to children expectations, attitudes, values and the like, both about themselves and about the other children in the class. Whether consciously or not, they thus provide a model of social relations. As a result they may help the development of prejudice, foster phenomena such as scapegoating, or even themselves display a kind of racism, possibly with the best will in the world or even while priding themselves on their even-handedness. Thus, it is apparent that appropriate preparation of teachers, development of suitable texts and other materials, and informed selection of content would all be part of a satisfactory response on the part of schools.

Why have schools been slow to respond?

Despite exceptions, British schools have in general been slow to respond to the presence in classrooms of increasing numbers of immigrant children, although the situation may well have improved somewhat in the last year or two, so that it should not be imagined that schools and related agencies are doing nothing. This slowness of response reflects a number of influences. At the purely logistical level, the immigrant presence has grown with astonishing rapidity, so that the schools have tended to be caught by surprise. For instance there were only about 8,000 immigrant children in London schools 25 years ago. Even 10 years later there were still only about 40,000, a fivefold increase to be sure, but still a number which could comfortably be absorbed without serious problems, except perhaps in a few schools where immigrants were concentrated. By 1972 the number of immigrant children in London schools had reached 140,000, and the figure stands at present at about 250,000. For the UK as a whole it is about 450,000.

The prevailing opinion is that schools can "tolerate" about 20 per cent immigrant children without their presence being perceived as a problem (Townsend, 1971). From a proportion of about one-third immigrant children, difficulties of the kind discussed in Chapters 2 and 6 become pronounced, and teachers and administrators see the school as having an "immigrant problem". Interestingly in this context, the British Government recommended to LEAs as early as 1965 that they should adopt a dispersal policy aimed at keeping the proportion of immigrant pupils in any particular class at or below the one-third mark, but only 11 out of 146 LEAs accepted this recommendation and adopted the dispersal policy (Taylor, 1974). In any event, the transition from the point where the number of immigrant pupils lay below the clearly "safe" lower boundary of 20 per cent to that at which it rose above the clearly "dangerous" upper level of one-third has occurred in most schools only very recently (if at all), despite the fact that there have been immigrants in Britain for many years. The transition thus overtook many schools as it were by stealth, and was therefore scarcely noticed until it emerged more or less fully developed. In other words, the need for "special arrangements" (Townsend, 1971, p. 5) has only recently become apparent.

Quite apart from the logistical question just discussed, a further cause of delay in the reaction of British schools has been the problem that there is no unanimity of opinion concerning what should be done (Townsend and Brittan, 1973). British primary schools have, according to Jeffcoate (1979), long had a tradition of sheltering or protecting pupils from the harsher aspects of the external world, so that, among other things a kind of "taboo on race" (Jeffcoate 1979, p. 14) has developed. Townsend and Brittan (1973) cited instances of headmasters and headmistresses who questioned the wisdom of special measures at all, on the grounds that their pupils knew nothing about race, and that raising the question in school would only make matters worse. Hopefully the discussions in Chapter 6 have made it clear that the sad fact is that difficulties already exist, even in the case of children in the lower grades, while the issue goes far beyond simply racism.

A related belief hindering effective action on the part of the schools is the prevalence of the opinion that the problem will simply go away of its own accord as immigrant and local children grow up together in the harmonious atmosphere provided by warm and accepting British primary schools. In the case of language, to take an example, it has often been assumed that there is no need for special provision, since the supposition is that young children simply "pick up" new languages quickly and effortlessly as a result of merely being exposed to them. Apart from the fact that it is actually an open question whether or not young children really are more gifted at language learning, this view fails to take account of the role of language in identity development and maintenance, as this role has been outlined in previous chapters.

By 1973 the Schools Council had published a report calling for *multiracial education* as a reaction to the presence of immigrant children in British schools. A 1977 Green Paper recognized that there were now stable communities of immigrants in this country, often with children born here, but retaining links with the homelands, and that their presence had implications for school curriculum. In particular it was emphasized that *all* children should be helped by their schooling to live in a multiracial society. In 1978 the Schools Council established a project on "multi-ethnic curriculum": it was emphasized that changes in British society have implications for curriculum not only in schools with a high proportion of immigrant children, but in all schools. In a 1981 report on this project, Little and Willey (1981) concluded that there is now widespread acceptance of the need for what they called *multi-ethnic education*. However, especially in schools with few or no immigrant pupils , this acceptance of the need for special provision has scarcely been translated into actual actions. It is important to notice at this point that the term "multi-ethnic" has a special significance in the present context: As Little and

Willey pointed out, its use marks a move away from the idea that adjustment of the British society to immigrants is primarily a matter of assimilation or absorption of the strangers until they disappear as the result of a process of homogenization, and acceptance of the fact that the society is now ethnically diverse and will remain so.

Recent publications such as those of Garrison (1981), although polemic in tone, make a strong case against the view that immigrant children should be treated just the same as white children. They contrast multi-ethnic education with the "mono-ethnic" education of the no-special-measures approach already discussed. Another publication (NUT, 1981) refers to the English language as the "enemy" of immigrant children, since it is both the language of domination by the white majority and also a link with a humiliating past — a symbol of alienation. On the other hand, mastery of English is recognized by many immigrant parents as essential for progress in the society of the UK. According to a press report of July 1st 1981, West Indian parents in Lambeth protested against a video film in which their children performed a play in West Indian dialect, demanding instead that the children be taught the standard, "good" English of the local society. Once again, the phenomenon of being between two worlds and in a double bind becomes apparent. The very title of the Garrison book mentioned above emphasizes this kind of problem, referring as it does to "identity crisis".

Some possible orientations for change

Weinberg (1976) identified three main "liberal" approaches to handling intergroup relations. The first is that of "tolerance": basically this approach, predominant in the USA in the 1920's, stresses that it is not acceptable to be unpleasant to outsiders (in the US case this meant Black Americans, but in the present context it could be understood as meaning Pakistanis and West Indians) merely because they are different.

After all, they have their rights too, and are probably actually very nice people. The second approach involves what Weinberg called the "interracial" attitude. The strangers are different but they are good at some things, better even than "we" are, so that it is clear that they have the potential to become more like "us". This approach has a liberal-humanitarian air to it, but is condescending and strongly oriented towards a form of integration involving absorption of outsiders into the majority group — a move towards national unity achieved through monistic assimilation. The third approach is based on a "human rights" orientation: all groups are regarded as of equal value, with different patterns of norms being seen as equally valid and as having a right to coexist with those of the majority group. This approach would accept what Smolicz (e. g. Smolicz and Secombe, 1977) called "ethnic coexistence". Put in plainer terms, the question at issue is that of whether immigrants should have to change in order to conform to British norms, whether Britain should change in order to make life better for immigrants, or whether something partway between the two is what is called for.

Approaches to assimilation in which immigrants are expected to fit in to the existing society, or else presumably go home or go under, have already been discussed in Chapter 5. Although the discussion will not be recapitulated here, it is certainly worth repeating that this approach has not been without problems anywhere, even in the USA, while modern experience (the Federal Republic of Germany offers an example which is close to Britain both in time and in space) suggests that it is now increasingly being found wanting, as well as being rejected on what might be called humanitarian grounds. Nonetheless, this approach has its champions: despite this, it is specifically rejected in the present book, on the grounds that it does not work but instead breeds discontent, conflict and social unrest (see Chapter 5 for a more detailed discussion).

It might also be expected that the other extreme position — that the responsibility for change should lie entirely with the majority society, in this case that the British should adapt themselves to the needs of immigrants without demanding any reciprocal adjustment on the part of the immigrants — would also be rejected out of hand. Interestingly, however, some writers have gone so far as to propose just that. Bagley and Verma (1975, p. 259) argued that Asian immigrants should not have to change in order to accommodate themselves to the ways of the British, but that the host community should be the one to change, if "natural justice" is to be achieved. It is hard to believe that these writers actually meant to be taken literally. Otherwise their standpoint could be parodied by claiming that they believe, for instance, that Urdu should become Britain's national language! Presumably their real intention was to state in a dramatic way the view that adjustment of immigrants also requires adaptation on the part of the receiving society — it is a give-and-take process, and not merely one in which the receiving society takes while immigrants give.

For the purposes of the discussion which follows, it is convenient to distinguish between measures aimed at helping immigrants to adjust to British life and measures aimed at helping the British adjust to the presence of immigrants. As will become apparent, these two categories are not necessarily mutually exclusive. Despite this, however, they will be treated separately here, in order to simplify the discussion.

Measures focused on immigrants — improved self-image

Measures focused primarily on immigrants can, again for ease of analysis, also be treated as having two thrusts which can be discussed separately, although once again they are not always mutually exclusive or contradictory. The first approach focuses on helping immigrant children overcome self-doubts, strengthen their faith in the worthwhileness of the values and norms of their original society, build a sense of identity, and so on. The measures adopted are, to use a term closely related to the theoretical analysis in earlier chapters, aimed at combating alienation or, to quote Jeffcoate (1979, p. 30), at promoting "racial self-respect". Among the strongest and most consistent representatives of this approach have been Verma and Bagley (e. g. 1979). The basic line of argument to which these authors have greatly contributed (although they should not be held responsible for the statements which follow), is that immigrant pupils experience a loss of clarity about their own identity, or even a sense of inferiority, shame, or rejection of their own background (see also Garrison, 1981). In the present book this has been described as encompassing various manifestations of alienation — alienation from their parents, from the receiving society, even from themselves (see Chapter 6 for a more detailed discussion).

The role of school in this alienation among immigrant pupils is complex. School is one of the most important, if not the most important socializing agency through which immigrant pupils are exposed to norms which challenge those of their mother country. It is also the place where their own differentness is probably brought home to them with the greatest force. Not only can they actually see their own differences from teachers and British children but, consciously or unconsciously, deliberately or accidentally, the schools make and transmit value judgements about what is right, what is wrong, what is good and what is bad, with the immigrants often representing the bad! This is done through content of lessons, through educational materials, and also through overt procedures such as evaluation of certain activities as desirable, others as incorrect or perhaps worse, odd, wrongheaded, intolerable, or wicked. The kinds of judgement which have just been mentioned also occur in the social sphere, with immigrants receiving feedback about their own outlandishness, being denied membership in prestigious or desirable social groups, even being openly rejected and made fun of, for example through the application of derisory labels such as "Nig-Nog" or "Fuzzy-Wuzzy".

School can thus be one of the prime causes of identity problems among immigrant children. This has led Verma and Bagley (1979) to propose that there should be active efforts in the schools to confront and eliminate phenomena such as racism, as well as the introduction of measures openly aimed at building up immigrant pupils' self esteem. This would involve what might be called "identity reclamation". The possible nature of such activities will be discussed more fully later — even a at superficial level, however, it is obvious that they could include elimination of negative stereotypes, giving increased emphasis to the positive contributions of immigrants' home countries to world history and the contribution of immigrants to life in Britain, and introduction of activities overtly aimed at promoting pride in their ethnic background among immigrant children.

However, not all commentators agree with the value of approaches having as their prime objective such "ethnic reinforcement". Apart from the fact that deliberate manipulation of pupils' self-image in order to foster a particular identity regarded as good by those doing the manipulation assumes alarming overtones of indoctrination if it becomes an overt goal of teaching, the contribution of ethnic reinforcement to the ability of the children in question to get along in the dominant British society must be questioned. The whole emergence of black prejudice against Whites in Britain, for instance, cannot unequivocally be regarded as a good thing. On the contrary, it may well represent a form of exaggerated ethnicity, encouraged by injudicious ethnic reinforcement, which is maladaptive for both immigrants and locals. Despite these misgivings, the fostering of racial self-respect seems to be a goal for schools which cannot be rejected out of hand. Nonetheless, as Jeffcoate (1979) argued, it may well be that this self-respect should arise indirectly out of carefully designed teaching, rather than being a direct objective of it.

Promoting qualities useful for life in Britain

The second approach focused on immigrant children aims at helping them develop knowledge, skills, attitudes, values and the like which will be useful for getting along in Britain. The purpose of such measures is to help the children "fit in" in Britain, or to put this more positively, to introduce them to British life and to factors which will make participating in that life easier (Townsend and Brittan, 1973). Unless it is assumed that some kind of system of apartheid, ghettoes, or voluntary separateness is going to develop in Britain, measures of this kind seem to be called for. Apart from basic knowledge of the three Rs, including mastery of the English language, a factor of such importance that it will be discussed separately in the next section, certain *values and attitudes* which frequently differ from those endorsed in many immigrants' mother countries are helpful, if not essential to successful adjustment to life in Britain. These include more individualism, independence, some degree of competitiveness, a willingness to make decisions for oneself, and so on. Thus, the development of these personal properties in immigrant children, or at least the development of the ability to cope with a society in which they are relatively prominent, is an important task for schools.

Unfortunately, but perfectly understandably on the basis of the discussions in Chapters 5 and 6, attempts to promote the development of personal characteristics appropriate to British ways may be opposed by parents, because the characteristics are often markedly at variance with the norms of the home country. Particularly in the case of girls, attempts to foster "British" values, motives and attitudes may thus actively be resisted by many immigrant parents, especially those of Asian origin. A special manifestation of this resistance to measures aimed at helping the development of personal properties likely to promote advancement in the British society sometimes occurs, paradoxically, when elements of the society and culture of the immigrant-sending countries actually are introduced into school curriculum. For example, Pakistani parents may welcome in principle the presentation of Muslim views as an addition to classroom activities in their children's schools, but may strongly resist the idea that this should be done in the critical way which is the ideal according to British educational thinking. Thus, the whole area of the promoting in immigrant children of attitudes, motives, values and the like which are more consistent with what is regarded as normal or desirable in Britain is more complex than at first seems the case. Among other things, the schools run the risk of increasing conflict between children and their parents, thus increasing adjustment difficulties, not reducing them.

Mastering standard English

Of the skills vital for getting along in Britain, probably the most obvious, and probably also the most crucial for social and economic advancement, is mastery of the forms of English understood and accepted in this country. At first glance talking of "standard English" or "the forms of English understood and accepted in Britain" seems to be excessively elaborate. However, the issue requires more discussion than might at first seem the case, as the difficulties experienced by West Indian children, who ostensibly speak English as their mother tongue, show. They often have more problems than Pakistani children, for whom English is clearly a foreign language.

According to Moses, Daniels and Gundlach (1976), there are five basic aspects of language. These are "intimate" language (this involves the linguistic symbols people use for reflecting upon their experience and may be fragmentary, ungrammatical and idiosyncratic), "casual" language (the form of language used for speaking with friends), "consultative" language (the form of language used for casual contacts with other people such as when ordering something in a shop), "formal" language (the form of language used when, for example, writing a speech) and "frozen" language (the form of language used when writing for publication — the use of language in this book is an example). The first language problem with immigrants is that they may have mastered English at only the first two or perhaps three levels, even when it is, in theory, their mother tongue. Schools, by contrast, place heavy emphasis on the fourth and fifth aspects, even when there is little likelihood that the children concerned will have much occasion in their later lives to use English for the kinds of purpose for which these levels are appropriate.

Steedman (1979) pointed out that each country usually has a "standard vernacular" (p. 261) language form. This is the language of government, education and the media. Once again, this is the form of English on which British schools concentrate. In addition, most languages have dialects based both upon geographical regions (for example the English of Cornwall as against the English of Yorkshire) or socioeconomic status (for example the English of the East End of London as against that of the Board Rooms of large national companies). Children may have extensive exposure only to dialect forms of the language, whereas schools concentrate upon use of the standard vernacular, and regard mastery of other forms as being of no significance, or even a sign of linguistic retardation, especially when the nonstandard forms are not regional dialects but forms typically spoken by immigrants. Honey (1983) has argued that the central problem in this area is not use of nonstandard pronunciation such as regional dialects, but use of nonstandard grammatical forms, since these make people's utterances sound quaint, odd, or even stupid, as well as making understanding difficult.

The difficulties associated with imperfect mastery of the English language are relatively obvious in the case of Urdu, Punjabi, or Pushtu speaking children, because English is clearly a foreign language for them. However, it is now being argued (see for example Steedman, 1979) that the failure to recognize that West Indian children speak a dialect of English rather than an inferior form of the standard vernacular has been the source of serious difficulties for these children. Whereas appropriate measures are frequently taken to assist Pakistani (and other Asian) children to acquire standard forms of English (e. g. through the provision of special classes, instruction in their native languages, etc.), it has generally been assumed that West Indian children's imperfect mastery of standard English must indicate that they are of inferior intelligence, since they are native speakers of English, and this is taken to mean the same form of English as that employed by teachers in Britain. In other words, whereas Asian children receive special support, West Indian children are classified as dull, and assigned to ESN classes (Townsend, 1971, Taylor, 1974, Bagley, 1979).

This "unfairness" has led to strong calls for recognition of West Indian Creôle as a legitimate form of English, a dialect in its own right (e. g. Jeffcoate, 1979). However, it is clear that mastery of standard English is an important prerequisite for progress in the British society. It is unrealistic to expect that the British will abandon standard vernacular English as the everyday form of the language, in favour of Urdu or Pushtu, or even a West Indian dialect! Thus, there seems to be little doubt that acquisition of the English language is important for immigrant children. Nonetheless, greater understanding of the socioeconomic and psychological dynamics of language acquisition and use is needed, along with better appreciation of the psychodynamic significance to immigrants of Asian languages or Creôle. This point will be discussed in greater detail in later sections.

Some approaches in Britain

In the early 1970's, as immigrant pupils began to appear in the schools in increasing numbers, especially in primary schools, two broad patterns of reaction emerged (Taylor, 1974). On the one hand was the laissez-faire approach based on the view, already mentioned, that nothing special need be done since immigrant children, being children and therefore flexible and adaptable, would quickly adjust. The British children, knowing nothing of prejudice, would quickly get used to the strangers and accept them. This view is of course rejected in the present book. The second reaction was that something had to be done — special arrangements were needed. These typically focused on teaching English to the newcomers, mastery of the local language correctly being identified as an indispensable prerequisite for successful adjustment to life in Britain. One example of a language-oriented programme is the Schools Council project *English for Immigrant Children*, published between 1969 and 1973. This is designed for children aged 8 to 15, and is intended for use with immigrant children in general, regardless of the original homeland. A similar Schools Council Project also published about 10 years ago is *Concept 7—9*. These materials were designed for West Indian children, and include special procedures aimed at compensating for the effects of West Indian dialect.

One common approach going beyond simply introducing new curriculum materials has involved establishment of special reception or language centres. Typically the centres were seen as providing an intensive introduction to the English language and to the fundamentals of British life. This introduction is usually packed into a very short period, so that the sojourn in the centres is a matter of about six weeks (Taylor, 1974). The idea is that immigrant children will then move on to normal classes, having acquired sufficient mastery of English and sufficient familarity with the basics of life in this country to permit them to get along in the schools. This approach has also been extensively employed in West Germany and found wanting there — experiences in that country are so informative that they will be reviewed more fully in a later section.

A second approach, where special provisions were made at all, has consisted of establishment of various kinds of special classes. These have usually involved withdrawal groups, the immigrant children being removed from the normal lessons for a certain portion of each day in order to receive special remedial instruction aimed at speeding up their mastery of the English language. In order to concentrate in one place enough children to permit establishment of such special classes, some authorities have collected immigrant children from several schools and brought them together for remedial English classes, thereafter returning them to their regular schools. Others have enrolled immigrant children in a single school in order to bring together a sufficient number of pupils to permit offering special instruction. Sometimes classes have been arranged after school, an approach which has the advantage that it avoids taking time away from normal instruction from children who, if anything, need as much time as they can get. However, such classes have the disadvantage that they can easily give the impression that the children in question are being punished by being given extra school hours, or at least create a feeling of being imposed on. Indeed, experience is that out-of-school classes are poorly attended by immigrant children.

Two measures focused on teachers can be mentioned here. Occasionally, provision for special language instruction for immigrant pupils has involved the services of peripatetic teachers who are, presumably, specialists in remedial English for non-native speakers. These teachers travel to different schools where there are immigrant children, giving special instruction in the English language. A related measure which has been little used in Britain is the employment of special teachers, peripatetic or fixed, who are themselves native speakers of the language of the immigrants in question — so-called "mother-tongue teachers". Both of these measures are increasingly being adopted in West Germany, the mother-tongue teachers normally being citizens of the country from which the immigrant pupils come, even in some cases being seconded from their native lands and retaining pension rights and the like.

There has been very little use in Britain of the mother tongue of the immigrant pupils as the language of instruction, with English playing the role of a foreign language. At first glance it may seem preposterous to propose that British schools should use languages other than English as the language of instruction. However, Cropley (1982) has argued strongly that, especially in the case of young children who at the time they start school have not yet mastered *any* language (mother tongue or English), this is often the best approach. The greatest likelihood for many children is that simultaneous exposure to two competing languages (mother tongue at home, English at school) will result not in bilingualism but in imperfect mastery of both (semilingualism). A chastening insight in this context is provided by the outcome of efforts in Sweden to achieve rapid mastery of Swedish and quick integration into regular Swedish schools of Finnish immigrant children. Despite enormous expenditures, the Finnish children have, in many cases, become merely semiliterate in both Swedish and Finnish (Paulston, 1978). This whole topic will be discussed more fully in Chapter 8.

Summarizing experiences on the Continent, Steedman (1979) concluded that short term, "crash" programmes to develop basic understanding of the local language in immigrant children, in the hope of then being able to absorb them into normal classrooms, do not work. Indeed, she concluded that not even a period of a year, far less six weeks, is long enough to achieve basic mastery of the local language. This has also been the experience in the Federal Republic of Germany, where short-term transition classes have not been as successful as had been hoped, and transition classes in the long form are now being introduced in several states.

In view of these experiences, the language centres in Bradford described by Khan (1977) seem to offer more promise. Children enter the centres in that city at about four-and-a-half years of age, and normally stay for one or one-and-three-quarter years, leaving at the age of six to enter normal schools. The centres aim at sending the children to school already possessing at least a working knowledge of English, thus minimizing their disruptive effects on the normal programme of instruction in the schools, as well as avoiding their segregation, or their identification as a "problem" group. The centres also have the advantage that they provide an intermediate experience in the transition of the children from a state of affairs in which they are mainly under the socializing influence of the home to one where home and school compete. The centres' less school-like, more family-like atmosphere hopefully eases this transition. Although seen here as a step in the right direction, even transition centres in the longer form will be shown in Chapter 8 to represent only a partial response to the real needs of the situation.

Experience in the Federal Republic of Germany

Although educational policy in the Federal Republic of Germany is a concern of the individual states, the existence of a federal coordinating body composed of representatives of the various states and the issuing by this body of guidelines means that, in effect, a *de facto* federal policy exists. The basis of this policy, as far as the education of children of foreign workers is concerned, presently rests upon two prime considerations. The first is that whatever measures are adopted should lead to the quickest possible integration of foreign children into the regular German school system. The second is that the national consciousness of the children, as well as their skill in their mother tongue, should be preserved and even fostered. It is very important to remember at this juncture that West Germany is, officially, not an immigrant-receiving society. Consequently, this humane-sounding policy should be understood against the background of the official expectation that the children will eventually return to their homelands. The preserving of the children's national identity is thus not merely a humane or altruistic matter, but is an essential aspect of the country's policy on foreign workers.

This policy seems, at least on the face of it, to deal directly with the two major issues — integration into the receiving society, on the one hand, guarding of identity, on the other. However, the facts of the matter are that very much the same kinds of problem, both in and out of school, have arisen in Germany as in Britain. These include high failure rates, behaviour disturbances, and high unemployment after the completion of schooling. Thus, there is no suggestion here that what is needed in Britain is adoption of measures now in operation in Germany. Nonetheless, educators in the Federal Republic have wrestled with the same kinds of problem as those in Britain, and some review of what they have tried is informative for British readers.

As in Britain, the early assumption in West Germany was that foreign workers' children would simply attend schools, where it was anticipated that they would rapidly pick up German, and quickly fit in. It was soon realized that inadequate mastery of the German language was a problem, and provision was made for special classes which children could attend for up to a year in order to develop knowledge of German before taking their place in the regular classrooms. By 1971 available provisions also included intensive courses in German during regular school hours, after school or in vacation periods. Later advances have included changed methods of assigning marks during foreign children's first two years at school in Germany (the system in the Federal Republic is still highly selective and each child's fate is highly influenced by marks, although the degree differs from state to state). Differences among groups of foreigners having special national characteristics are now more frequently recognized and, of great importance for the present discussion, instruction in the various mother tongues as first or second foreign language, as well as use of the foreigners' mother tongues as languages of instruction, is becoming more common. By 1976, instruction in the mother tongue was available, although on somewhat differing bases, in several states. In other words, the mother tongues of the foreign workers were receiving clear recognition as important elements in carrying out the twofold policy outlined earlier.

One approach to the teaching of the mother tongue has been to teach it as a supplement to the usual syllabus through voluntary classes sometimes held during normal school hours at the expense of other subjects, sometimes after school. Teachers are native speakers of the language in question, usually professional teachers from the mother country. Results have not been particularly good. Only a few children attend the classes which, in any case, frequently conflict with teaching of the regular syllabus. In grammar schools the various mother tongues can be offered as options for study as first or second foreign language. However, since, as in Britain, few foreign workers' children find places in academically oriented streams, this approach hardly affects most of the children concerned.

Much more comprehensive than simply offering the mother tongue as a subject of study is its use as the actual language of instruction. The best known German approach of this kind is the one seen in the state of Bavaria. An important feature of the socalled "Bavarian Model" is that children of foreign workers commence their schooling in their mother tongue and not in German. Wherever 25 children with the same mother tongue are collected in the one school they may be consolidated into a single class (a "national class"), and instruction carried on in their language. Teaching is done by native speakers of the language in question; in 1977 there were 400 such teachers in Bavarian schools, and the number was rising rapidly. German is taught as a foreign language for at least eight hours a week, and in subjects where language is not a crucial element the children may be taught in German, in the company of German children (eg. sport, handwork). If the children develop mastery of the German language sufficiently, they can, if they wish, leave the mother tongue classes and enter a conventional classroom. However, they may continue to receive instruction via the mother tongue. This provision would probably be widely regarded as nonsensical in Britain, where it is clear that the strangers are immigrants rather than visitors. The crucial element of this approach is that the children are under no formal pressure to acquire German and integrate into the German society. In theory at least they could spend many years in Germany without ever learning the language. The positive feature of the model is that it could be expected to facilitate maintenance of "racial self-respect". The weakness is that it does little to foster acquisition of crucial skills for coping with life in Germany.

By 1977 more than one third of all foreign workers' children in Bavaria were being taught in this way. According to Mohr (1977), the results have been favourable. Parental interest in school has been higher than previously, there has been less truancy, and marks have improved. The mother tongue classroom children have also done as well in German as immigrants in regular classrooms, although this is largely a reflection of the fact that both groups do poorly. Nonetheless, the Bavarian approach has been much criticized (e. g. Rist, 1978), mainly on the grounds that it promotes a kind of apartheid, and that the longer foreign children take their schooling in the mother tongue the more difficult it will be for them ever to master German and ultimately be integrated into German society. To date it has not become universal in Germany, although some other states have moved in a similar direction. In Nordrhein-Westfalen, for example, a similar programme is now in operation, although there is more teaching in German, mathematics for instance being taught in that language.

The second approach in West Germany is typified by the "Berlin Model". This city is already experiencing a tendency for Turks in particular to cluster in suburbs such as Kreuzberg, a word which is now almost synonymous in Germany with "ghetto". In some schools in this part of the city, by September 1979 every child commencing the first grade was a foreigner, and few spoke German! West Berlin is cut off from the rest of Western Europe and is thus restricted to a specific small area with literally no room for foreign quarters. Not surprisingly, therefore, the thrust of the Berlin approach has been to achieve the quickest possible assimilation of foreign children into normal German classrooms. The emphasis is thus on rapid acquisition of the German language.

The Berlin approach follows a dispersal policy of the kind recommended in Britain in 1965, but mainly ignored. An attempt is made to ensure that there are never more than 20 per cent of immigrants in any class, the remainder being of course German. Foreign children having the same mother tongue are not concentrated together, even among this 20 per cent, although the tendency for members of different nationalities to live close to each other may mean that one or two mother tongues predominate among the minority group of foreign children. Foreign children are, if possible, immediately placed in a German classroom at a level commensurate with their age and the level of schooling already reached in the mother country (if they have been to school there). Where their inadequate knowledge of German makes it necessary, they may receive intensive German instruction, usually during normal school time when they are released from lessons in other subjects to concentrate on German. This approach has the great disadvantage that it reduces the amount of instruction received in other subjects, precisely in the case of children who are already experiencing difficulties. When command of German is so seriously deficient that placement in a normal classroom is completely out of the question, the children can be placed in a transition class for up to 18 months. The purpose of these classes, however, is not to develop mastery of the mother tongue, but to build a command of German good enough to permit placement in a regular classroom with 80 per cent or more German children.

The differences between these two German models show very clearly two contrasting approaches to the schooling of foreign children. In Bavaria the children are deliberately concentrated together, preferably with native speakers of their mother tongue. In Berlin they are deliberately dispersed. In Bavaria the mother tongue is the language of instruction in the early years, the schools deliberately promoting its development and seeking to add German on as a supplementary language. In Berlin, German is the language of instruction and the aim is unequivocally mastery of German, the mother tongue being at most something which the children use "on the side". The Bavarian approach is strongly multicultural, the Berlin model strongly assimilationist. Liberal opinion in Germany clearly favours the Berlin approach. In other words, the predominant attitude is assimilationist. The Bavarian model is seen as exploitative and rejecting, with the real motives for fostering retention of mother tongue and national identity being the desire to keep foreign workers in an inferior position where their deficient assimilation will ensure that they remain a social underclass and a source of cheap labour. At the same time they can always be expelled from the Federal Republic if the economic situation becomes acute. These are not, of course, the goals of the model as stated in official documents, but are those imputed by many observers (e. g. Rist, 1978, reflecting the common opinion).

Unfortunately no clear cut data exist for assessing the effects of the two approaches. Supporters of both point to various positive effects, but opponents, especially of the Bavarian model, offer sharp criticisms. The true motives of the politicians and educators involved need not be discussed here, although it must be admitted that they are very interesting. Supporters of the assimilationist approach, in personal discussions, refer repeatedly to the danger of the development of Harlem-like ghettoes in Germany, or to the cruel disadvantages suffered by members of perpetual outsider classes, seeing these dangers as outweighing the alleged benefits of a multiracial society. Public opinion and official policy are, in any case, quite clear that the Federal Republic is not an immigrant receiving country, despite the continuing presence of over four million foreigners, many of whom have either been in the Federal Republic for many years or, increasingly, have been born there, and the fact that over 9 per cent of all children unter 16 are now foreigners. This discrepancy between policy and fact hampers most discussions in West Germany. What the two German models do, as far as the present book is concerned, however, is demonstrate some of the differences between an approach aimed at achieving the quickest possible assimilation for foreigners (i. e. of the use of schools to adapt foreign children to the local ways), and one which does not press for such assimilation, and which would promote the emergence of a multiracial society (even if not designed with this in mind).

Measures focused on British children

As Steedman (1979) pointed out, in a review of provisions for children of foreign workers in Western Europe, the adoption of measures aimed at adapting the outsiders to the local system does not normally eliminate the problem. Also needed are measures focused on children of the majority society. To put this somewhat differently, it is also possible to think about the educational response to immigrant children by considering not what to do with or for the newcomers, but how to alter the education of the majority in order to help them cope with the presence of the minority (Verma and Bagley, 1975). In various writings on this topic Bagley has presented the issue as primarily a matter of eliminating prejudice on the part of the Whites. He has, in fact, gone so far as to praise alienated behaviour on the part of immigrants, such as refusing to accept work and living instead on the dole, on the grounds that this reaction (to what he sees as racial prejudice in the society) preserves personal integrity and dignity better than accepting an inferior occupational, economic and social status.

Following the line of argument that the major factor needing to be dealt with in the majority society is racial prejudice, the changes needed in schools, as far as the education of the majority is concerned, are then seen as having to do with changing attitudes in order to eliminate prejudice. Bagley and Verma (1975) have advocated a direct attack through the introduction of activities having the specific purpose of changing attitudes. On the other hand, Stenhouse (1975) has argued that the task for schools is not to seek directly and unilaterally to change attitudes; although schools have a definite role in the making and changing of attitudes they are only one of many contributing factors. Schools should concentrate on crystallizing the issues (for example by specifically identifying the existence of prejudice, and promoting pupils' understanding of the phenomenon, how it develops, what factors maintain or support it, what effects it has on both groups involved, etc.).

In the Centre for Applied Research at the University of East Anglia, Stenhouse and his co-workers have studied three approaches or techniques for crystallizing the issues and promoting understanding of them in school children. Material on prejudice could be introduced into social studies lessons in a relatively standard, formal way; through "units" or "topics" such as "Race Relations in Britain", etc. The topic of prejudice could also be introduced in drama studies — depiction of incidents involving prejudice, the precursors and consequences, and the like. Finally, he has suggested the "neutral chairman" approach. The teacher assigns specific projects touching upon prejudice in the society, and the pupils prepare materials. A discussion then takes place in which the pupils introduce evidence and discuss and evaluate it. The teacher introduces the topic and keeps order, but otherwise takes no sides and does not control the opinions offered during discussions. Verma and Bagley (1979) have extended the Stenhouse approach by arguing in favour of a "didactic" role for the chairman. The didactic chairman would not merely introduce the topic and keep order, but would play an active role in "exposing" and "discrediting" racism. In the same book, these authors compared the effectiveness of the acting out or drama approach, the neutral chairman method and the didactic chairman technique. They reported that both of the latter two produced significant reductions in racial hostility displayed by white schoolchildren. Nonetheless, some critics of such approaches have argued that prejudice is already present in pre-school or younger school children, so that remedial measures would have to start very early. This means that Stenhouses's methods, even as extended by Verma and Bagley, are not practicable, in the sense that they are suitable for use only with somewhat older children, and would thus be confined to shutting the stable door after the horse had bolted.

Adapting the entire curriculum

Emphasizing the goal of "social accommodation", in which both newcomers and long-term residents adapt to each other, Saunders (1980) sees education as having as one of its goals the removing of impediments to mutual adjustment. This would require not merely language instruction for newcomers, but reform of the entire curriculum — as Jeffcoate (1979, p. 4) put it, it would require a "total response" of such a kind that the whole curriculum would be " 'permeated' with a multiracial 'constant' ". Dargent (1978) goes further, and calls for a reorganization of the educational system itself. However, when one considers the fate of the Schools Council-sponsored project *Multiracial education: Curriculum and context*, possibly the most celebrated curriculum development in this direction, there are grounds for a certain pessimism. Finished in 1976, the final report had not been released for general publication by early 1980, being withheld on the grounds that it was too controversial. Thus, it is necessary to ask just how far the society is really prepared to go in accepting curriculum changes of the kind called for by many writers.

Although not developed specifically with an eye to the presence of immigrant children in schools, the Schools Council supported project *World Studies 8—13* provides some valuable guidelines which indicate the kind of broad themes which would need to be emphasized in lesson content aimed at promoting peaceful coexistence between immigrants and long-term residents. Among these themes (see Hicks and Fisher, 1982) are: *Similarities and Differences; Values and Beliefs; Conflict; Social Change; Distribution of Power; Fairness; Co-operation; Interdependence; Communication.* These are themes which are capable of being introduced into many different subject areas. The goal of their adoption, or of adoption of similar general principles, is to introduce into all aspects of school studies an increased understanding of the legitimacy of differences among groups, a willingness to tolerate such differences and an openness to change in society. Further suggestions for changes in the classroom will be made in Chapter 8.

8
Conclusions and Suggestions

Need for special measures

The first issue is whether anything special needs to be done in the schools at all. For example many people believe that children simply "pick up" languages and that, if left alone, immigrant children in Britain would be no exception. In a similar way, it is expected that they will become true Britons as a result simply of living here. It is also argued that prejudice is found only in adults, and that British and immigrant children who grow up together in the schools will not become racist. Finally, there is the view that it is better to leave the whole thing alone, as interfering will only make matters worse. A particularly interesting version of this latter approach, and one which gives much food for thought, is the idea that a small amount of ill-conceived exposure to anti-racist measures only serves to make children immune to the effects of a full scale attack on racism — the "innoculation effect" (Miller, 1969). Townsend and Brittan (1973, p. 13) have cited a good example of a typical statement to the effect that the whole issue is best left alone: "Continuous discussion of racial differences in culture and tradition serves only to perpetuate them".

The research on language acquisition by immigrant children in other countries has already been mentioned in several places. Although this theme will be discussed more fully in following paragraphs, the findings suggest that learning the local language can be a difficult task for some immigrant children. Practical experience in Britain makes it clear that many children are not in fact successfully "picking up" an adequate mastery of the forms of English which dominate in British

schools (e. g. Nicol, 1974). The belief that there is no prejudice among children has been attacked by both Jeffcoate
(1979) and Bagley and Verma (1975), who have shown that
prejudice is present in young children, and that there is "a depressing amount" of it in British schools (Bagley and Verma ,
1975, p. 258). Finally the belief that discussion of racial differences should be avoided, because it only makes the situation
worse, has been rejected by Verma and Bagley (1975, p. 299)
in very strong terms; they called it "horribly wrong".

The position adopted here is that there is a clear need for
special measures. These can be conceptualized as embracing,
on the one hand, activities aimed at helping the locals to accept immigrants, on the other, procedures aimed at helping
immigrants get along in Britain. These latter measures include
developing in immigrant children the skills needed to adapt
successfully, developing appropriate attitudes, values and
motives, and helping them to come to terms with their own
identity as people caught between two worlds. The present
chapter will concentrate on measures aimed at helping immigrant children function in the real world of British society.
The line of attack will be mainly concerned with combating
identity problems (i. e. alienation, especially alienation from
the self, self-doubt, uncertainty, deprecation of one's own
skin colour or ethnic background, etc.). It should be noted
that this approach differs from some other recent discussions
in that it sees immigrant children as the main "recipients" or
focus of the measures suggested. Many other discussions have
suggested school approaches whose main aim is to "expose"
or "combat" racism, and have thus focused on Whites. Such
activities are no doubt important, while some of them can
serve both ends, tending to combat white racism and also to
reduce identity conflicts in immigrant children. However, the
present book is more concerned with the psychological development of immigrant children rather than, say, eliminating
racism.

Schools cannot solve societal problems on their own. The
"problem" is located not only in schools, but also in family,
church, clubs, peers, media, even government and bureau-

cracy, so that there is need for changes in the whole social system (Stenhouse, 1975). Jeffcoate (1979) has reinforced this view by pointing out that even school-based activities are complex in their operation. The effects of interventions aimed at combating racism depend not only on the content of lessons, but also on the kind of relationship that exists between pupils and teacher in a particular classroom, the styles of learning adopted, the patterns of communication in the room, as well as on the general "racial climate" (p. 41) of both school and surrounding neighbourhood. Nonetheless, schools are in a position to make a major contribution, probably even to take a leading role.

Problems in mastering the English language

Little (1975) and other writers have emphasized the importance of helping immigrant children achieve mastery of standard English. Despite the earlier prevailing opinion that the children would pick up English as a result merely of exposure to it (Taylor, 1974), without the necessity of adopting any particular measures, various procedures have already been developed. For youngsters who are not attending school, these include day release from work to permit attendance at language centres, government-supported classes in works and factories, and classes run in youth clubs and similar organizations. Although the present argument is that this approach is not sufficient, it is clear that organizational measures for giving young people access to learning opportunities are to be commended. Another out-of-school approach, this time preschool, is the language centres such as those in Bradford which have already been mentioned. The idea here is that young children (four-and-a-half- and five-year-olds) attend in order to learn enough English to start school at the normal age and in normal classes.

One defect of these approaches, however, is that they fail to go far enough, for example not going beyond rudimentary English to second stage English (Townsend, 1971). Another improvement in special provisions for helping immigrant children to master standard English would be to recognize that there is a considerable degree of linguistic diversity among different groups of immigrant children, as well as variability from child to child within groups. This suggests the importance of offering language instruction to homogeneous groups of children who have the same needs and difficulties (Steedman, 1979). It also raises the question of differences between Pakistani and West Indian children. West Indians frequently need remedial English rather than English as a foreign language (i. e. they can speak English, but they use nonstandard forms). Many Pakistani children, by contrast, need second stage English (i. e. the English they know may be standard, but they may simply not know enough).

However, more is needed than minor improvements like the ones just suggested, valuable though they may be and, indeed, adequate for the needs of many children. One important phenomenon has been described by Paulston (1978). Some children, when learning a new language or a new version of the old one, "lose" the mother tongue faster than they acquire the new one or, to put it slightly differently, they give up the old language or language forms without acquiring compensating new ones at the same speed. The result can be, not bilingualism but "semilingualism". One factor which favours this phenomenon is the absence of out-of-school experiences promoting acquisition of the new language (in this case English). The problem may thus be particularly acute for children who do not speak English at home (many Pakistanis), or children of low socioeconomic status (a high proportion of West Indians). These children do not receive the same degree of language support at home as most middle class children, partly because of the lower ability of some parents to model appropriate language behaviour (according to the norms of the schools), partly because of lower interest in language on the part of parents and children, not to mention the various physical disadvantages such as crowding which have already been described.

Even more important for the present analysis is the "ego-dynamic" role of language (Titone, 1978, p. 291). As has been emphasized in several places, language is not simply a neutral communications device, but is also a major factor in the formation and maintenance of identity. It is a crucial instrument for obtaining and interpreting information, a major factor in expressing and perceiving emotions, and the medium of unconscious or subconscious processes. It contains built-in predispositions to react to people and events in certain ways (i. e. it influences attitudes), is the vehicle of much of a people's culture, identifies the members of a society to each other and also indicates approximately their social and personal relationship (for example by showing that a speaker is a fellow member of the working class or of the middle class, etc.), provides a strong sense of belonging and of group membership, and is a medium through which a people expresses its sense of national identity, national pride, solidarity, and the like (for example through speeches, songs, stories, plays, books, laws, etc.). To cast off a language and take up another is thus considerably more than to change clothes or, to use a language-related metaphor, to switch to a new typewriter. Despite this, it is clear that a very large number of people learn new languages, mostly without experiencing intrapsychic disasters. Bilingualism is, in fact, probably the normal state of affairs for a majority of the world's people. Many Pakistani immigrants are already bi- or multilingual when they arrive in Britain. Why then should learning standard English pose such problems for many immigrant children?

Resistance to learning English

Two concepts from the literature of bi- and multilingualism are helpful in considering the question just posed. The first concerns the difference between "elitist bilingualism" and "folk bilingualism" (Paulston, 1978, p. 311). Elitist bilingualism is the state of affairs prevailing when a person learns a second language as a result of making a personal choice — because it is an interesting thing to do, gives access to foreign writings, is a mark of high culture, makes vacations more fun, and so on. This is usually the kind of bilingualism involved when British children learn French or German or other languages at school. The second kind of bilingualism, folk bilingualism, occurs when people learn a new language because they have little or no choice in the matter, since they must acquire the new language if they are to survive (usually economically and socially rather than in the literal sense). This is the kind of bilingualism seen in immigrants who acquire the language of the receiving society, not because it is fun or the cultivated thing to do, but because they have to.

The second important concept centres on the difference between "substitutive" and "additive" bilingualism. The latter form of bilingualism occurs when the new language is acquired as a supplement to the original one. There is no question of the new language replacing the mother tongue. When a British child studies, say, French at school, the number of cases in which the child and its parents expect that this will eventually lead to the abandonment of English as the child's day-to-day language is probably so small as to be virtually non-existent. This means, of course, that most cases of elitist bilingualism presuppose that the relationship between the mother tongue and the new language will be additive in nature. By contrast, substitutive bilingualism, as the term implies, involves learning a new language which will eventually replace the original language (in the present discussion, the mother tongue). Efforts in the receiving society to promote learning of the language of that society by immigrant children often raise the suspicion in the minds of the people concerned (especially parents), that the phenomenon of "glottophagie" (Calvet, 1974) — the devouring of one language by another — is being set under way. Once again, there is a relationship between substitutive bilingualism and the earlier distinction between folk and elitist bilingualism, because substitutive bilingualism almost always occurs in people who learn the new language because they must do so in order to get along in life.

What this means is that the learning of English or of local forms of English by immigrant children is, in many cases, a different matter from the taking of 0-Level French or German by a British child. English is learned not from choice but from grim necessity, while there is a very real danger (when the matter is looked at from the point of view of immigrant parents) that acquisition of English by children will be accompanied by loss of the mother tongue. The "rhetoric of the return" is important here, too. The more strongly immigrant parents believe that the family will eventually return home, the less they are likely to welcome loss of the mother tongue. As a result, to put it mildly, measures for promoting the learning of English will not receive the unqualified support of immigrant parents if the parents feel that the measures are the first step towards glottophagie. Once again, a stumbling block is placed in the way of immigrant children.

Looked at in terms of the internal psychological processes involved, it can be seen that the acquisition of English can be regarded as a crucial step in abandoning the values, attitudes, social relations and mores of the mother country, as well as being a major step towards abandoning a personal identity based on the norms of the homeland. In other words, approaches to the teaching of English which give the impression that the mother tongue is to be replaced invoke the double bind which has been discussed earlier. This is particularly true when it is borne in mind that the norms of British society include rejection of immigrants, and that the English language is the instrument of such rejection. This is the case not merely in the sense that racist statements in Britain are frequently made in English, but also in the sense that the language is the instrument of ego-dynamic functions, as they have just been described, which include prejudice, discriminatory attitudes, racism, and the like. The more English is actually adopted and internalized, the more immigrants have to accept or even support rejection of their own background. A simple example of this at a superficial level is the existence in fluent, everyday English of expressions such as "nigger in the woodpile". The attitude towards Blacks hidden in this innocent phrase is obvious. In a sense, then, to learn English is, for some immigrant children, to reject oneself.

Despite what has just been said, it is clear that learning English really is one of the most important, probably the most important, task for immigrants, and especially immigrant children. To imagine a British society with five or six official languages is, in my view, unrealistic. Personal experience of living in a country with two official languages (Canada) where large blocks of the populace are, nonetheless, unilingual, suggests that the absence of a single national language spoken by all (even if there are also minority languages) is a nuisance, as well as having economic and social disadvantages. What is needed, then, is measures for promoting acquisition of the English language among immigrant children without this process leading to alienation or self-rejection.

Bagley and Jeffcoate have both recently discussed the learning of English by immigrant children in the United Kingdom. Bagley (1979) concluded that little attention is actually being paid to language as a crucial factor, despite the existence of some special measures such as those which have already been mentioned earlier in this chapter. Jeffcoate (1979) has gone a step further, recommending not only that the teaching of standard English should be an important measure for immigrant children, but urging that this should be done in a way which avoids deprecating the languages or accents of Pakistani and West Indian children. In the terms used in the present book, he has urged avoiding making rejection of the mother tongue or dialect (alienation from the old society) the price of acceptance as an English speaker.

Role of the mother tongue

The comments of the writers who have just been mentioned are certainly a step in the right direction. However, the analysis developed in earlier chapters, supported by international research on the acquisition of the local language by immigrant children, suggests that a much stronger line is called for. Paulston (1978) has reported some striking data involving immigrant children from Finland in Sweden. Despite expenditure of a great deal of money, efforts to help these children to master Swedish have been strikingly unsuccessful when judged against the expectation that the children would quickly learn Swedish if given a certain amount of systematic encouragement and support. Finnish children who came to Sweden at the age of about 10 have succeeded in achieving a form of bilingualism involving normal mastery of both languages. Those who moved at about age 12 have also learnt Swedish while maintaining Finnish, although the acquisition of Swedish has taken longer. Children who came to Sweden prior to school age or who moved to Sweden after about one year of schooling in Finland did worst of all. These results were attributed to the absence of a sound linguistic base in the mother tongue. Paulston (1978, p. 325) concluded that for many children the first necessity is to master the mother tongue:

The evidence is perfectly clear that mother tongue development facilitates the learning of the second language, and there are serious implications that without such development neither language may be learned well, resulting in semilingualism.

This line of argument suggests that the first step in learning the language of the receiving society should be mastery of the mother tongue. This, in turn suggests, in the early years, that emphasis in schools should be on teaching immigrant children their mother tongue. Indeed, Paulston has made precisely this point, summarizing the argument for the view that "teaching children in their mother tongue is a more effective way of teaching them the national language". The suggestion that languages such as Urdu or Punjabi or West Indian dialects should be studied in British schools would probably be at least tolerable to many people. However, the idea that they should become the language of instruction would probably be rejected out of hand by most. Nonetheless, in the very early stages such as kindergarten, there is a case to be made for, at the very least, promoting respect for immigrant children's mother tongue. It is important to notice that instruction in the mother tongue is not necessarily the preferred strategy for all immigrant children — however, in those cases where there is hostility to the new language or fear that the mother tongue will be lost, or where the children are of low socioeconomic status and receive limited linguistic support at home, it seems to be particularly necessary to take account of the mother tongue, especially in early years.

Cropley (1982) has argued that this is because such children otherwise fail to develop a general language orientation (interest in using words, positive attitude towards language, ability to manipulate abstract symbols, "feel" for the communication possibilities of language) with the result that the language of the receiving society is learned badly, as well as the original mother tongue. Cummins (1976, p. 37) has referred to a "threshold level of linguistic competence" which is a prerequisite for acquiring a second language, and which comes in most cases from mastering the first. The crucial point is that children who learn that language is an area of life fraught with problems, for instance because the language spoken at home is a sign of ignorance, stupidity or, at the very least otherness, or because the majority language is seen as hostile and threatening, are in danger of developing negative feelings about language as a mechanism for dealing with the world, or else of exaggerating their allegiance to the language of otherness, as seems to be the case with many West Indian youngsters. The result can be failure to develop the language orientation already mentioned, or retreat into an exotic dialect which serves perfectly well for communication in a small circle of acquaintances, but restricts opportunities in the larger world. In both cases, mastery of standard English is likely to suffer — attitudes in the community at large to the "foreign" language of the home, or in the home to the majority language, translate into a state of psychological unreadiness to acquire one or other form of "standard" English. The problems arising from this state of affairs go beyond simply the relegating of language to a low-status position in the value system of many immigrant children, however. As Paulson (1978) has pointed out, negative attitudes to language and associated low levels of ability or willingness to deal with the external world in the differentiated, symbolic terms made possible by language impede development of other cognitive skills, especially the kind which are necessary for school success. The result is that, even in the absence of any fundamental intellectual weakness (i. e. even in the case of children whose intelligence is perfectly normal), school success is blocked.

It is clear that many immigrant children are in precisely the situation where the danger is greatest that they will fail to acquire this language orientation or not reach the threshold. They are often of low socioeconomic status, come from homes where the parents cannot provide appropriate models of the use of standard language forms, and often face rejection and discrimination which are linked to the English language. They not infrequently come to school in Britain at a point where they have not yet mastered the mother tongue, and are then expected to acquire a second language (English), despite the fact that they have not reached the "threshold" or do not possess a favourable "orientation". It is scarcely surprising that some of them experience difficulties with the language.

Thus, it is suggested here that considerably more provision be made in Britain during the early school years for emphasis on the mother tongue. In contrast to the popular view that children will "pick up" English, the most serious problem lies with younger children. If any group can "pick it up", it seems to be children aged 10 and above when they come to Britain. If any group needs particular help, it is the children born in Britain who come from home backgrounds where linguistic levels are lowest and where alienation from the British society is greatest.

Two important points must be made here. The first is that many immigrant children clearly learn English very well. Hopefully, however, the remarks which have just been made will suggest systematic differences between those who do and those who do not, thus permitting more differentiated treatment of immigrant children, rather than regarding them as a homogeneous group. The second is that there is no intention here of proposing that Urdu or Pushtu or Punjabi or Jamaican Creôle should replace English, nor that immigrant children should be discouraged from learning English. Emphasis on the mother tongue is recommended because it will facilitate the acquisition of standard English. Even more importantly, this approach has good potential for fostering a state of affairs in which the norms of the British society and those of the mother country work together, rather than in opposition to each other. Indeed, the use of the various mother tongues is regarded, as might have been guessed from previous sections, as a key to achieving assimilation to the British society with minimum alienation from the homeland, not just for children, but for adults too.

One of the strongest recent attacks on the teaching of non-standard English, for instance creôle, is to be found in the work of Honey (1983). He rejects the view that other forms apart from standard vernacular serve just as well, as long as people can make themselves understood, pointing out that among other things, people who cannot speak standard forms are unable to present their point of view in convincing ways. This means that teachers who fail to teach their pupils standard English are "emasculating" them, and condemning them to the "language trap". He criticizes substitution of creôle for standard English as a deception: it may conceivably enhance the self-esteem of black children, but it condemns them to a state of perpetual alienation from the mainstream British society. For this reason, black parents who insist that their children be taught standard English are voicing a wise demand.

Avoiding alienation is not only good for the well-being of the British society, but it is also a humane approach when the negative effects of alienation are kept in mind. Nonetheless, this approach will probably find only limited acceptance, especially when the socio-political aspects of the situation are kept in mind. In West Germany for instance, emphasis on the mother tongue is rejected out of hand by one political party, on the grounds that it is politically unacceptable. The encouragement of the mother tongue in one *Land* is attributed by many commentators to a desire to keep foreign workers' children in the position of second class citizens (i. e. non-speakers of German). Nonetheless, some writers in Britain are now

calling for more use of the mother tongue in early grades
(e. g. Verma and Mallick, 1978).

Multicultural schooling

Although language, both English and the mother tongue, is
an important factor in promoting an accommodation between immigrants and receiving society, provisions focusing
exclusively on language run the risk of becoming mainly "cos-
metic" (Cross, Happel, Doston and Stiles, 1976, p. 6). This is
because most people would agree that it is good for immigrant children to learn English, because extra lessons and similar measures are highly visible and relatively easy to organ-
ize,and because even modest progress is easy to demonstrate
or even makes itself obvious as children begin to speak English. Language instruction is therefore attractive for those
charged with doing something about "the problem". However, approaches aimed at fostering development of English
language skills in immigrant children, although important,
are inadequate as the sole response to fostering adjustment of
immigrants and locals to each other.

What is needed is a much more comprehensive approach.
As has already been mentioned, this should really go beyond
simply school based measures, and include procedures in the
society as a whole. At the level of schools, nonetheless, there
is need for a comprehensive approach encompassing what
Steedman (1979, p. 261) called "multicultural" schooling.
Such schooling would include provisions for the learning of
English and, hopefully, would also take much greater cogni-
zance of the importance of the mother tongue. However, it
would require a more comprehensive restructuring of school
curriculum, and not merely special language courses and the
like. Existing approaches have tended to concentrate on eliminating racism (see Chapter 7). However, the danger of the deliberate adoption by teachers of a crusading role aimed at
stamping out unacceptable thinking should not be ignored.
The danger is the introduction of authoritarian teaching
methods which reduce multicultural teaching to the status of

"indoctrination" (e. g. Jeffcoate, 1979, p. 29). The desire to promote positive relationships between immigrant and white pupils needs to be expressed in ways which are still consistent with the promotion of freedom and plurality of opinion, and with the fullest self-development of pupils, not merely with improving the lot of immigrant pupils. This statement is not, however, meant as an excuse for ignoring racism or even encouraging it in the name of freedom of opinion, but as a counterbalance to some writers who have recently written as though schools should openly be used for propaganda purposes.

To some extent, school activities which make available to different social groups more information about each other are a first step in the direction of promoting mutual tolerance. However, neither contact alone, nor information alone (Jeffcoate, 1979) eliminates prejudice. Jeffcoate gives a good example of this difficulty. He describes a study in which a group of British children wrote essays showing knowledge about Asian folkways, even appreciation of them. The same children, however, still concluded that Asians should be repatriated to wherever they had come from. Another issue in considering the relative importance of approaches based on presentation of aspects of the culture of the immigrant-sending countries is that of whether cultural issues really get at the fundamental problem. As Weinberg (1976) put it, what immigrants really want is good jobs, good housing and admission to friendly relationships with the majority society, rather than success in converting the receiving society's citizens into admirers of the cultural achievements of the country of origin. In any case, as the Jeffcoate example cited a few lines earlier shows, appreciation of culture does not necessarily lead to the disappearance of prejudice. What this means, then, is that measures based on presentation of information about the immigrant-sending societies and depiction of life there in a positive light should not have, as their main purpose, merely the transmission of information or even the winning of interest among the local children. These alone are not sufficient.

For the purpose of the present analysis, the most important purpose of teaching about immigrants' mother countries, apart from the goal of fostering tolerance and respect in the British (which, as has just been argued, is nice but not enough), is to promote the adjustment of immigrants to life in this country. This does not mean that its purpose is to encourage monistic forms of assimilation, an approach which has already been criticized in Chapter 5. The aim is to build immigrant children's understanding of the relationship of the lifeways of their mother countries to those in Britain, to promote their understanding of the process of adjustment to a new society, and to help avoid the destruction of their self esteem — to use the language of earlier chapters, to avoid alienation. Appropriate contents and methods would also be expected to affect the British children too, of course, and despite what has just been said this aspect of multicultural schooling should not be ignored or undervalued.

Content of lessons

The immediate reaction to discussion of the need for curriculum with a multicultural orientation is to think of the implications of such an orientation for content — what subjects are taught and what material is introduced into lessons on these subjects. An obvious example of a possible reaction is the introduction of "Black Studies" programmes. Such programmes usually contain material on history, economics, ecology, culture and so on of immigrant-sending countries. However, they have several shortcomings. They do not always address themselves to the core problem of helping with jobs and the like (although this is not in itself a fatal criticism, since otherwise multicultural schooling would be reduced to the discussion of how to get work), they take time away from the study of skills which may be more central to getting along in Britain (such as English or mathematics) if focused on life in the homelands, and they may have limited concrete relationship with life in Britain. Thus, Black Studies is likely to be a fringe or "soft" option at a time when immigrant pupils need "hard" material. Black Studies are a clear example of what Jeffcoate (1979, p. 41) called "overtly multiracial" approaches. In addition to the shortcomings already listed, such approaches "tend to yield counterproductive effects" (p. 41) by annoying white pupils and by embarrasing Blacks.

Despite what has just been said, there is a place for immigrant-oriented content in school curricula. The need for such multicultural content varies from school to school, for example because of differing proportions of immigrant children in different schools. There are also differences in the extent to which schools feel it necessary to introduce multicultural material in different subject areas. In a survey conducted about 10 years ago Townsend and Brittan (1973) found that the subjects where there was the greatest felt need for such material were religious education, humanities and English. These were also, not surprisingly, the subjects in which the greatest amounts of multicultural material had been introduced. This finding certainly makes sense intuitively, as it indicates that the strongest felt need and the most pronounced school reaction was in the areas of curriculum most closely related to culture, values, norms and the like.

However, as Townsend and Brittan (1973) pointed out, many other disciplines offer opportunities for the introduction of multicultural content, including history, geography, social studies, science, physical education, art, domestic science, etc. Possible topics which could either be introduced into these subjects or else handled in a somewhat different manner include race relations, apartheid, discrimination, group and interpersonal relations, religious beliefs, even genetics. Particularly obvious is the introduction into social studies or geography of studies of the immigrant-sending countries, in the present case especially Pakistan and the West Indies. Topics could include themes such as housing, schooling, social customs, religion, dress, food, holidays and festivals, games and sports, even attitudes to animals. To some extent, since projects based on specific countries are already often used in subjects such as social studies, it should be possible to introduce this kind of material without engaging in excessive propaganda and without becoming annoyingly "overt".

More specific discussions of the possibilities have been given by Townsend and Brittan (1973) and Verma and Bagley (1975). In the case of English for example, reading materials could be chosen to include topics such as prejudice, intolerance, deprivation, race problems, and so on. Indeed, many set books already touch upon these themes, although some teachers may avoid them or seek to minimize the extent to which the themes are specifically confronted. Supplementary reading could also be chosen to include less obviously racial or even political material, for example books and stories based on myths and legends of Asia and the Caribbean. In the case of language activities, discussions and debates, as well as plays selected to be read or acted, could either deal with multicultural topics or could include materials by or about Pakistanis and West Indians. Jeffcoate (1979) has given examples of how this can be done, and what may be expected to emerge. An important proviso, however, is to avoid using these materials for propaganda or preaching. Not only is this approach repugnant on the grounds that it is bad for schools and schooling to become openly instruments of indoctrination, but also because it is boring or embarrassing for pupils.

To take another example, the teaching of history could be altered to a certain degree without necessarily introducing new topics — i. e. without drastic changes in content. The history of Britain could be taught as the continual adaptation of newcomers and earlier inhabitants to each other, and the emergence, in many cases, of a society differing from either of the earlier ones. The very development of the English language is an example of this process. Events in colonized lands after contact with the British could be taught partly from the viewpoint of the colonized, and not only that of the colonizers. The Afghan wars in the mid 1800s, to take an example with continuing relevance, would have a somewhat different look when seen in the context of struggles on the part of Afghanistan (whose people are largely speakers of Pushtu, the native language of many Pakistani immigrants) to remain independent of both Russia and Great Britain, while at the same time being divided by internal conflicts. Similarly, study of the effects of great world leaders on history could include reference to Asian and African leaders, and not merely Greeks, Romans and British. Finally, history could be presented as the study of how various groups of people have struggled to develop and protect their own way of life, and how they have adapted to conquest, oppression and the like.

Other subjects too offer good opportunities for the orientation of content in the direction of multiculturalism, sometimes without even the necessity of introducing new areas of study, but merely by choosing material on a somewhat different basis. An obvious example is music, and the suggestion which springs to mind at once is Reggae music. Asian music too could be introduced into lessons. Art is a similar subject where the possibilities spring quickly to mind, with good chances to look at Asian and West Indian paintings, models and artifacts in a respectful, accepting way (rather than presenting them as examples of what the darkies are capable of, or as cute because of their exotic nature). Batik materials, masks, puppets, tie-dyed cloth, and so on, are other examples.

A related subject is home economics where, again, the prospects are good. Not only can unfamiliar food materials be introduced into lessons, but in addition this subject offers opportunities to discuss organization of the family, child rearing and discipline, food preferences and preparation, use of fabrics, fashions and colours, and so on. It should be remembered that the traffic here should not all flow in one direction — discussion of family life or food taboos and the other topics just mentioned can serve not merely to give British children more information about immigrants, but can also serve to introduce immigrant pupils to British ways. Even physical education offers opportunities for immigrant children to learn values of the British society such as the ideal of fair play, with the chance of increasing the respect of British children for their immigrant fellows and of building their own self-respect. An anecdote from real life shows the possibilities here very clearly. At the age of nine an Australian boy was introduced to a former Pakistan test cricketer. In a patronizing way the boy asked the cricketer, "Did you ever play against Australia?", showing by his manner that he expected to be able to gloat over the superiority of his countrymen. "Yes," came the reply, "and we beat you!" The boy looked covertly at the man at every chance thereafter, astonishment and new-found respect clear on his face. He had never realized before that Pakistanis were supermen! (Unfortunately, the more recent facts of Test cricket have now penetrated the consciousness of even Australian expatriates.)

Multicultural perspective

Discussions to this point have been oriented towards content, although not necessarily suggesting manipulation of content to the point at which the multicultural orientation becomes "overt". Rather, what has been proposed is retention of the accepted curriculum, but with selection of topics, themes, specific examples and the like in a way which emphasizes multiculturalism. However, an equally, perhaps more important problem is the way in which content is presented. Indeed, it may well be that the problem is not so much exclusion of material on other cultures, but the perspective from which these cultures are presented. It is not so much a problem of suitable content, then, but of appropriate methods. A central defect of much material is that the standpoint is extremely ethnocentric (e. g. Jeffcoate, 1979, p. 35). The task is to break away from stereotypes (Cross, Happel, Doston and Stiles, 1976). What is needed is teaching about other cultures which emphasizes their legitimacy (Steedman, 1979), or shows that differences between peoples are interesting, even worthwhile (Cross et al, 1976). In the case of immigrant pupils, this would mean that the norms of British society can and should be taught (they need to know how things are done in this country), but that a groundwork of the kind just described will hopefully make it possible for this to take place in an atmosphere of tolerance and respect for their original culture, not one of rejection. In other words, accepting British norms would not be seen as a capitulation or a rejection of those of parents and the old country, but as the perfectly legitimate action of fitting in with an alternative system. Similarly, acceptance of the norms of the UK would not mean acknowledging that the previous ones were wrong or stupid, and hence that the elements of the identity based on the original country are inferior — i. e. it would not require the kind of identity clash which has already been portrayed as a major problem for immigrant children.

What this means in more practical terms has been sketched out by Jeffcoate (1979). He argues for the retention of traditional themes, but with a change of perspective in the content offered, not a new content. For instance, examples, illustrative materials and the like in many subjects could be drawn partly from the cultures of immigrant pupils, not merely from traditional sources. Such material would need to be introduced as though it were normal, rather than comical or quaint, avoiding the Oxfam and Tarzan images which have already been discussed. As Jeffcoate put it (p. 33), the material would need to be "extensive", "accurate", and "unstereotyped". He has suggested ground rules for how to change the orientation of lesson content in the desirable direction. Material presented should:

    (a) Be international in orientation;
    (b) Reflect a variety of levels of society and of ethnic groups;
    (c) Contain accurate information about race;
    (d) Avoid stereotypes;
    (e) Avoid judging other cultures and races by British standards.

Learning materials

Changes of the kind already outlined would require, or at the very least be greatly helped by, the development of appropriate learning materials including books, films, tapes, slides, posters and similar learning aids. One problem which has been emphasized by both Bagley and Verma (1975) and also Jeffcoate (1979) is that of ethnocentric or even downright racist text books. Such materials can find a place in classrooms even in the total absence of any intention to discriminate or be prejudiced. The example mentioned earlier of the teacher playing with a toy house shows how bias can creep into lessons. Unfortunately, the suggestion that biased, ethnocentric or racist materials should be avoided or even eliminated raises the whole issue of the extent to which teachers should place themselves in the position of censors, ferreting out any teaching materials which they deem to be racist. Whether the elimination from the classroom of "Ten Little Nigger Boys" or "Taffy was a Welshman" is a triumph for racial equality or a piece of humbug is not so easy to determine. This is an issue which needs to be thrashed out. In addition to essentially negative actions, however, there is also a positive role for teachers through the choosing of texts and supporting reading or other teaching aids which reflect ethnic diversity, deal with racially sensitive topics in a useful way, and so on.

One possible area where supportive materials might be developed or modified involves psychological, achievement and aptitude tests. In this domain, there may well be a place for procedures which would help in identifying both pupils with special potentials masked by difficulties of the kind described in Chapter 6, as well as for materials capable of detecting special needs or difficulties. Of particular interest in this context would be tests or other procedures for distinguishing between children who were truly educationally subnormal, those who had merely had inadequate opportunities to develop language, and those whose problem was basically simply inadequate mastery of standard English. This sounds so obvious as to be a truism. However, experience has shown that many children whose difficulty is merely of the latter sort are wrongly treated as subnormal and placed in inappropriate settings. It may also be claimed that appropriate procedures are already in widespread use. However, the kind of thing meant here is not simply new versions of existing tests, but new approaches.

The procedures developed by Schubert and used with Canadian Indian and other children (e. g. Schubert and Cropley, 1972) are an example of one approach which might well be extended. The procedures are based on the notion that intelligence is primarily a matter of the ability to process abstract information using language as the processing tool, and that the appropriate verbal skills which constitute intelligence are obtained by children through their social interactions with adults. Using a test apparatus which requires subjects to solve problems involving the displaying of lights in various colours and positions, the procedure measures the extent to which children are able to regulate their behaviour through the use of verbal symbols. Absence of this ability is then shown to stem either from a true lack of the capacity for such control or from simply lack of the experiences which foster its acquisition. The latter state of affairs may well be the situation of many West Indian children presently treated as educationally subnormal.

Teaching and learning methods

In this area many possibilities come quickly to mind. These could include discussions of plays and stories with immigrant-oriented themes. The whole matter of discussion methods has already been treated in Chapter 7. In addition, other possibilities include clubs or working groups which would collect materials on immigrant-sending countries and make presentations to classmates. The content could be something straightforward such as, say, stamps from Pakistan. A related activity would be the undertaking of out-of-the-classroom activities by mixed groups of locals and immigrants, such as camps or excursions. These activities could include visits to schools with an unusually high proportion of immigrant pupils and discussions of the problems encountered and measures adopted in such schools. Representatives of minority groups could be invited to give talks to classes, not only representatives of well-known immigrant groups such as Pakistanis and West Indians, but also people from other outgroups such as North American Indians, Palestinians, Turks from West Germany, and so on.

Teachers and teacher training

The need for teachers capable of giving instruction in the various mother tongues has already been mentioned. One possible source of such teachers is the homelands from which the immigrants have come. At a time of job shortage in the United Kingdom the suggestion that more teachers be imported is hardly likely to win much support. However, the possibility of recruiting teachers from among immigrants already in Britain does not seem to be out of the question. A drive to recruit and train mother tongue teachers would also be a move in the direction of integrating immigrants into the more socially prestigious levels of the British vocational structure. Blomqvist and Åstedt (1977) have discussed the qualifications and qualities required of mother tongue teachers. They would need, of course, total mastery of the mother tongue of the immigrant pupils whom they would teach. In addition, they would have to be completely fluent in English. Even more importantly, they would have to be thoroughly familiar not only with the norms of the immigrant sending country with which they were concerned, but also with those of the English society. The latter would need to include familiarity with Britain's laws, with people's rights and privileges, and so on. Finally, they would need appropriate personal qualities such as patience and teaching skill, and above all a strong sense of identity which would permit them to "get outside" their own socialization in order to function in a truly multicultural way.

Since the number of British teachers who are fluent in Urdu, Pushtu and Punjabi, not to mention Jamaican Creôle or the languages of other immigrant groups, is low, it seems likely that most if not all mother tongue teachers would themselves be immigrants. However, there is also a strong need for British teachers with special qualifications in multicultural teaching. These people would also need the personal properties mentioned in the previous paragraph, plus insight into the whole issue, for example as it has been explained in the present book, and skill in presenting content, choosing materials, and designing activities of an appropriate kind. A particular group of such teachers would be specialists in the teaching of English as a foreign language.

The call for specialist teachers possessing the necessary knowledge and skills implies, of course, appropriate training (e. g. Commission for Racial Equality, 1978). Recognition of the importance of teacher training in this area is, however, by no means new. About 10 years ago Abraham (1974) called for special forms of teacher training, to take one early example. Interestingly, Abraham made the point that teachers should not be trained simply to heap praise on the way of life of migrant-sending societies — although this might help immigrant children to have more respect for their own backgrounds, while increasing their status in the eyes of British children, it involves scarcely more than attempting to substitute one stereotype for another. As Abraham pointed out, teachers should be encouraged to draw attention to aspects of life in the homelands which are difficult to justify or would be rejected in a wide variety of societies, or which are in the process of changing. Immigrant children thus need to develop a certain degree of scepticism about some features of their homelands, as well as an awareness that these societies are subject to a process of change. As he points out, however, this requires a good deal of tact, or it will lead to clashes with parents. The whole area of teacher training has taken on new importance in the light of the 1983 White Paper on improving the quality of teachers in general. Better teacher education is seen as a crucial element in this process, and major changes are envisaged.

In the present context, substantial improvements in the preparation of teachers for work in a school system serving a multicultural society are called for. This could, however, take the form of either preservice or inservice training, the present oversupply of teachers suggesting that inservice training would be particularly suitable. In a recent publication, Craft (1981) supported the view that teacher training is essential if systematic implementation of a curriculum appropriate to a multicultural society is to be achieved, but also made the point that this requires in turn extensive training of personnel in the teacher-education field — training of the teacher trainers. At present, however, very limited growth is being seen in the provision of teacher education of the necessary kind. A recent survey carried out by members of Her Majesty's Inspectorate indicated that fewer than 15 per cent of public teacher-training institutions in Britain had recently improved their offerings in the area of immigrant education, while about 45 per cent were of the opinion that multicultural issues have no relevance to teacher education. In other words, the point made by Craft seems to be particularly important: the first step is to convince teacher training agencies, since it seems clear that a widespread increase in teacher expertise in the area of multicultural education will only occur if appropriate teacher education is made available. However, development of teacher education in the desired direction can only occur when a rationale, theory or model of what is required has been developed. It is hoped that the present book will make a contribution to the development of such a rationale.

The contribution of kindergartens

The kindergarten is, for many children, the first point of contact between home and school; it is the place where they have their first systematic experience of secondary socialization. Kindergartens are thus capable of functioning as a bridge or intermediary between the narrow world of the family and the broader world of the society outside the home. In the case of immigrants, an important part of this contact is exposure to the English language or to the forms used in the wider community. If it has not already begun, training in English commences at this point. In some countries kindergartens have been seen as the most important point in the process of acquiring the language of the receiving society. In Scandinavia, for instance, great emphasis has been placed on the provision of training in Swedish or Danish or Norwegian, as the case may be, from a very early age. However, as will be remembered from earlier remarks, this has not eliminated problems of inadequate mastery of the language in question.

However, kindergarten is more than a place for acquiring skill in the local language. It is the first stage in the second phase of socialization, the point where experiences within the family begin to be integrated with those in the larger society. It is a source of many experiences which children simply cannot have at home, such as relating to strangers and adult authority figures, learning to get along with peers, acquiring membership of peer groups and, particularly important for immigrant children, learning the norms of the receiving society as against those of the narrower environment of the home. As the meeting point between primary and secondary socialization experiences, the kindergarten is of great importance in the present context: it is the point where the two worlds meet, more or less head-on, for the first time.

This means that experiences in kindergartens can set the pattern for attitudes to school and indeed to the majority society as a whole. If the norms of British life are presented as a rival to those of the home, the earlier ones are likely to be seen as inferior because of the prestige the local norms have by virtue of being the dominant ones. The result may, in many cases, be confusion (which of the competing sets of norms is actually right?) or rejection of those of the home, with the consequences of alienation, adoption of defensive tactics such as exaggerated ethnicity, acting out, and the like. Thus the emphasis should be on cooperation between school and home, on building upon experiences within the family as the basis for psychological development, rather than correcting earlier patterns of socialization. In other words, the kindergarten can make a vital contribution to establishing for immigrant children a pattern of cooperation between primary and secondary socializing agencies similar to the one which exists in the case of local children. One measure which has already been discussed in detail, and will only be mentioned here, is the use of the mother tongue as the language of instruction, or at the very least, as a subject for instruction.

Measures focused on parents

Competition between school and home is not the result only of rejection of immigrant children's primary socialization experiences by schools. Not infrequently immigrant parents make a lesser contribution to achieving the necessary reconciliation than they might, or even actively encourage rejection of the norms of the receiving society. Thus, one necessary measure is the development of approaches focused on parents. A failure of parents to make their contribution to the avoidance of alienation may reflect not only rejection of British norms, but may also stem from anxiety or uneasiness about becoming involved in what goes on in schools because they are regarded as strange or frightening places, from apathy or lack of interest, or even from simple ignorance of the possibilities. It may also reflect a feeling of helplessness or incompetence, or fear of contact with people in official positions.

Thus, there is need for provision of a kind of counselling for immigrant parents. This could be carried out by specialized social workers or by liaison teachers. Both of those measures already exist in the United Kingdom, but there is room for considerably greater development through the training of more personnel and through better training. Other kinds of work with parents could include provision of instruction in English, especially intensive initial instruction, provision of programmes on housekeeping or shopping or other areas of interest to parents, and discussions with mother tongue speakers of the possibilities and difficulties in the schools. Use could also be made of immigrant newspapers in the mother tongue, particularly for informing parents about the schools, getting them to work with the schools, and so on.

An important action with regard to parents would be getting them involved in the life and work of the schools. In Britain serious efforts have already been made to involve immigrant parents in the actual teaching process, for example by using them as voluntary helpers or as resource people for special topics such as the history, economy, geography or daily life of their homelands. In Denmark in particular a drive has been made to get the parents of immigrant pupils involved in the administrative and planning side of schooling, for example by adding immigrant parents to membership of school boards, thus giving them a stronger voice in the construction of syllabi or the development of programmes, even an influence on the educational philosophy of their children's schools. A serious effort in this direction in Britain is called for.

Measures focused on the community

Just as family and school need to work together in a more cooperative way in order to reduce competition between socializing experiences — to bring the two worlds closer together — there is also need for actions aimed at increasing cooperation between home, school and larger community. One fairly obvious example of the possibilities in this area centers on such activities as language clubs run after school by local groups, using both English and the appropriate mother tongues, and involving both British adults and also adult immigrants. These could include, in or out of school time, discussions or talks on topics such as the contribution of immigrants to the local community. Immigrant bus conductors or doctors could talk about their work, passengers or patients, both coloured and white, could discuss their contacts with immigrants, British workers could talk about their relationships with coloured colleagues, and so on. Other possibilities include undertaking by immigrant children of "social work" programmes in which they would visit sick or elderly locals, or in the reverse direction, activities in which British children would work with immigrant families. An example here would be the use of older British children as "tutors" for younger immigrant pupils.

An interesting action of the kind just discussed has been described by Cropley (1982). Residents of a German town have developed a programme for providing help to "problem" immigrant children which has a strong community base. The scheme is financed partly by the local educational authority and partly by the parish. Schools identify "problem" children and pass on their names to the coordinators. These children are then linked up with a German, usually a full-time house-wife, who acts as a tutor and counsellor. The scheme was developed by the local community on the basis of public meetings and discussions at which immigrant parents were also present. Meetings were bilingual or even multilingual so that foreigners felt less inhibited by their lack of skill in German.

Other possible actions of a related kind include establishment of multicultural centres to foster contacts between immigrants and Britons, both adults and children, under conditions of mutual respect rather than on an ingroup-outgroup basis. This kind of approach could be supported by presentations, both within schools and also in the community at large, of cultural activities of immigrants such as singing and dancing, ceremonies to mark national days or famous historical events, and so on. Some of these events would, of course, be shared by Pakistanis, West Indians and Britons because of the overlapping cultural background they possess. Of great importance in this context would be the proviso that the presentations should not be presented as curiosities, but as interesting examples of how to carry out the activities in question, which have an interest beyond their exoticness or unfamiliarity.

Research and development

The first necessity in this area is probably a much clearer official policy on relations with immigrants. In the present context this would mean establishing a policy with regard to assimilation, and an attitude to the norms of the mother countries. Are the immigrants here to stay? Are they to become British at all costs? Is Britain to become a multicultural society or is the pattern of assimilation to be monistic? Is there a place for languages other than English in British schools and in the community at large? Is the government prepared to adopt massive measures aimed at facilitating the adjustment of immigrants to Britain, and to accept the associated expenditures? The answers to these kinds of policy question are not as obvious as might seem to be the case. It is easy for educational psychologists to make pronouncements on what is best, but they do not have to decide what other areas will suffer cuts in order to find the necessary money, nor do they have to take the overall responsibility for the results of the actions they recommend. Nonetheless, a coherent educational policy seems to be a major need.

With or without a guiding policy, substantial development activities are needed. These include the working out of an approach to the teaching of English to students for whom it is not the mother tongue. Approaches to teaching English as a foreign language already exist, of course. The problem, however, is that they tend to be oriented towards the development of elitist bilingualism — i. e. to assume that the students actively desire to learn English, admire the language, do not feel threatened by it, and have appropriate social backgrounds, home supports, etc. A problem with immigrant children is that many of them may be hostile to English, may feel threatened by it, may have parents who either do not help or even actively resist the use of English, and may come from home backgrounds where both attitudes and values, as well as physical conditions, are not conducive to good language learning. What is needed, in a nutshell, is the development of an approach to the teaching of English which is specifically designed for alienated children, in the sense that the term has been used in Chapter 6.

Despite considerably increased recent interest in the area, it is apparent that there is still need for extensive investigation of the processes which have been outlined in earlier chapters, and of the best approaches to solving the problems. A simple example would involve testing whether the various measures suggested in earlier sections really do have the beneficial effects they are thought likely to achieve. An interesting methodological point has been made by Tsiakalos (1978) in this connection. He criticized existing research on the grounds that it is "external": the issues are looked at from the point of view of the receiving society, not from that of the immigrants. What is needed is "internal" research. He gave the example of kindergarten education. To the British, kindergarten is a good opportunity of introducing children to the world of school, and of breaking them in to this world by stages, as well as a device for building basic skills in the children and ultimately improving their later school performance. To some immigrants, by contrast, sending children to kindergarten may be a sign that the family is incapable of providing proper care at home. (Tsiakalos was writing in the context of immigrants in West Germany, and gave the specific example of Greek rejection of kindergarten. Nonetheless, the example is also understandable in a British context.) It is apparent that "internal" research which revealed the negative attitude just outlined would suggest a somewhat different approach to persuading immigrant parents to send their children to kindergarten than would external research which judged refusal in terms of British norms.

The argument that an internal research approach is needed does not mean that all other research should be abandoned. What is needed is a broadening, not a switching from one narrow form to another. Among the more traditional research needs are the tryout and evaluation of methods for the teaching of English, as well as the development and testing of appropriate aids and materials and teaching methods. This would require specifying the goals of any such measures and the development of criteria for ascertaining if those goals had been reached. For example, is the aim of special measures that of making immigrant children fit in and cause no trouble, or of developing a multicultural society? As has already been mentioned, these are largely policy questions, but they need to be enunciated clearly by researchers, and subsequent actions need to be evaluated accordingly.

Emphasis on programmes with a strong community orientation suggests that there is a need for the development of alternative forms of child care and preschool programmes, including kindergartens, and for alternative forms and methods in preschool and early school education. This is especially true in the case of the role of the mother tongue at these levels. The present book has argued that this role should be greatly strengthened and has argued that certain benefits would flow from this approach. However, the question is ultimately an empirical one and should be treated as such. Similarly, measures for involving parents in schooling, developing more favourable attitudes in parents, linking schools with the community, and so on, need to be developed and assessed. Finally, the whole process of assimilation and alienation needs to be worked out in more concrete terms, facilitating and inhibiting factors identified, and appropriate strategies and specific activities developed and tested. As a single abstract guideline for such activities the principle is offered here that primary and secondary socializing agencies should not contradict each other, but should work together in order to fuse the "two worlds" whose competing and conflicting existence has been identified as the crucial psychological factor in the adjustment of immigrant children to life in Britain.

Closing thoughts

Two surveys, published about 10 years apart, have already been mentioned in earlier sections of this book. The first was Townsend's review of "the LEA response" (Townsend, 1971), the second Little and Willey's (1981) review of "the way forward". Happily, Little and Willey were able to report that there had been a drastic change in attitudes in LEAs between the two surveys — the need for special provision was widely accepted, not only in the form of activities for immigrants but also for all children. However, when they made direct comparisons between Townsend's recommendations (plus their own perceptions of what is needed) and the actual adoption of concrete measures, the picture was rather different. Lack of agreement on the nature of the "problem", competing priorities, lack of expertise, and similar problems continue to hamper the development of a really systematic attack on the whole situation. The 10 years between surveys had not brought all that much concrete progress. It is hoped that the present book, although ending on a pessimistic note by drawing attention to the continuing uncertainties plaguing workers in the area and the often disappointing lack of apparent progress, will make a contribution to conceptualization of the problem and development of appropriate responses.

References

Abraham, A. S. (1974) 'Time to Help the Underdog', *Times Educational Supplement*, September 27th, p. 23

Akpinar, U., Bendit, R., Lopez-Blasco, A. and Zimmer, J. (1978) 'Sozialisationshilfe für Ausländerkinder', *betrifft: Erziehung, 11*, 38—50

Anderson, C. C. and Cropley, A. J. (1966) 'Some Correlates of Originality', *Australian Journal of Psychology, 18*, 218—227

Bagley, C. (1972) 'Deviant Behaviour in English and West Indian Schoolchildren', *Research in Education, 8*, 47—55

Bagley, C. (1975) 'The Background of Deviance in Black Children in London' in G. K. Verma and C. Bagley (eds.), *Race and Education across Cultures*, Heinemann, London (a)

Bagley, C. (1975) 'Sequels of Alienation: West Indian Migrants in Britain' in K. Glaser (ed.), *Case Studies in Human Rights*, Nijhoff, The Hague (b)

Bagley, C. (1979) 'A Comparative Perspective on the Education of Black Children in Britain', *Comparative Education, 15*, 63—81

Bagley, C. and Verma, G. K. (1975) 'Inter-Ethnic Attitudes and Behaviour in British Multiracial Schools' in G. K. Verma and C. Bagley (eds.), *Race and Education across Cultures*, Heinemann, London

Bagley, C. and Verma, G. K. (1979) *Racial Prejudice, the Individual and Society*, Saxon House, Farnborough

Bagley, C., Bart, M. and Wong, S. (1978) 'Cognition and Scholastic Success in West Indian 10-Year-Olds, a Comparative Study', *Educational Studies, 4*, 7—17

Bagley, G., Mallick, K. and Verma, G. K. (1979) 'Pupil Self-Esteem: A Study of Black and White Teenagers in British Schools' in G. K. Verma and C. Bagley (eds.), *Race, Edu-*

cation and Identity, Macmillan, London

Ballard, R. and Ballard, C. (1977) 'The Sikhs: The Development of South Asian Settlements in Britain' in J. L. Watson (ed.), *Between Two Cultures*, Blackwell, Oxford

Berry, J. W. (1970) 'A Functional Approach to the Relationship Between Stereotypes and Familiarity', *Australian Journal of Psychology, 22*, 29—33

Bhatnagar, J. K. (1970) *Immigrant Children*, Cornmarket Press, London

Blomqvist, K. and Åstedt, I. (1977) 'Einwandererkinder in der schwedischen Vorschule', *Aktuelle Informationen aus Schweden*, Whole No 165 (June)

Bloom, B. S. (1964) *Stability and Change in Human Characteristics*, Wiley, New York

Bogardus, E. S. (1949) *Sociology*, Macmillan, New York

Brah, A. (1978) 'South Asian Teenagers in Southall', *New Community, 8*, 47—55

Brody, E. B. (1970) 'Migration and Adaptation' in E. B. Brody (ed.), *Behaviour in New Environments: Adaptation of Migrant Populations*, Sage, Beverly Hills, California

Brown, L. and Selznick, P. (1955) *Sociology*, Harper and Row, New York

Calvet, L.-J. (1974) *Linguistique et colonialisme: petit traité de glottophagie*, Payot, Paris

Christopher, L. (1972) 'Nottingham: West Indian Education in Crisis', *Race Today*, (June)

Coard, B. and Coard, P. (1971) 'A West Indian Child's Real Problems', *The Guardian*, March 10th, p. 10

Collard, D. (1970) 'Immigration and Discrimination: Some Economic Aspects' in *Economic Issues in Immigration*, Institute of Economic Affairs, London

Commission for Racial Equality (1978) *Schools and Ethnic Minorities*, Commission for Racial Equality, London

Cropley, A. J. (1982) *Erziehung von Gastarbeiterkindern: Kinder zwischen zwei Welten*, Ehrenwirth, Munich

Craft, M. (ed.) (1981) *Teaching in a Multicultural Society: The Task for Teacher Education*, Falmer Press, Lewes

Cross, D. E., Happel, M., Doston, G. A. and Stiles, L. J.

(1976) 'Responding to Cultural Diversity' in D. E. Cross, G. C. Baker and L. J. Stiles (eds.), *Teaching in a Multicultural Society*, Free Press, New York

Cummins, J. (1976) 'The Influence of Bilingualism on Cognitive Growth: A Synthesis of Research Findings and Explanatory Hypotheses', *Working Papers on Bilingualism*, 9, 1—43

Dahya, B. (1974) 'The Nature of Pakistani Ethnicity in Industrial Cities in Britain' in A. Cohen (ed.), *Urban Ehtnicity*, Tavistock, London

Dalby, R. O. (1972) 'The German Private Schools of Southern Brazil: German Nationalism v. Brazilian Naturalization', *International Review of Education, 18*, 391—397

Dargent, A. (1978) 'Scolarisation des enfants immigrés', *Aprés-Demain*, No 204—205 (May-June)

David, H. P. (1970) 'Involuntary International Migration' in E. B. Brody (ed.), *Behaviour in New Environments: Adaptation of Migrant Populations*, Sage, Beverly Hills

Deslonde, J. (1976) 'You Know the Rules!: Myths about Desegration' in D. E. Cross, G. C. Baker and L. J. Stiles (eds.), *Teaching in a Multicultural Society*, Free Press, New York

Dove, L. (1975) 'The Hopes of Immigrant Children', *New Society*, 32, 63—65

Driver, G. (1980) 'How West Indians do better at School (especially the Girls)', *New Society, 51*, 111—114

Egger, E. (1977) *Migrants' Education*, Council of Europe, Strasbourg (Council of Europe Document CME/x(77) 5

Eisenstadt, S. N. (1954) *The Absorption of Immigrants*, Routledge and Kegan Paul, London

England, R. (1929) *The Central European Immigrants in Canada*, Macmillan, Toronto

Fitzherbert, K. (1967) *West Indian Children in London*, Bell, London

Foner, N. (1977) 'The Jamaicans: Cultural and Social Change among Migrants in Britain' in J. L. Watson (ed.), *Between Two Cultures*, Blackwell, Oxford

Garrison, L. (1981) *Black Youth, Rastafarianism and the*

Identity Crisis in Britain, ILEA, London

Goutman, R. (1977) 'Educational Administration's Hidden Priority', *International Review of Education, 23*, 129—131

Hammet, J. (1965) 'Marginality and Mental Health', *Australian Journal of Social Issues*, 2, 18—26

Hansen, M. L. (1940) *The Immigrant in American History*, Harper and Row, New York

Harris, M. (1962) 'Morals and Manners' in P. Coleman (ed.), *Australian Civilization: A Symposium*, Cheshire, Melbourne

Hicks, D. W. and Fisher, S. (1982) 'World Studies 8—13: A UK Curriculum Project', *International Review of Education, 28*, 499—504

Hiro, D. (1971) *Black British White British*, Eyre and Spottiswoode, London

Honey, J. (1983) *The Language Trap: Race, Class and the "Standard English" Issue in British Schools*, National Council for Educational Standards, Venton, Middlesex

Hurrelmann, K. (1979) 'Erfolg und Versagen in der Schule', *forschung: Mitteilungen der DFG*, No 4, 19—21

Jansen, C. J. (ed.) (1970) *Readings in the Sociology of Migration*, Pergamon, Oxford

Jeffcoate, R. (1979) *Positive Image: Towards a Multiracial Curriculum*, Chameleon Books, Richmond

Jeffrey, P. (1976) *Migrants and Refugees*, Cambridge University Press, Cambridge

John, A. (1971) *Race in the Inner City*, Runnymede Trust, London

Jones, C. (1977) *Immigration and Social Policy in Britain*, Tavistock, London

Jupp, J. (1966) *Arrivals and Departures*, Cheshire, Melbourne

Kavass, I. (1962) 'Migrant Assimilation', *Australian Quarterly, 34*, 54—66

Keniston, K. (1965) *The Uncommitted: Alienated Youth in American Society*, Harcourt, Brace and World, New York

Khan, V. S. (1977) 'The Pakistanis: Mirpuri Villagers at home and in Bradford' in J. L. Watson (ed.), *Between Two Cul-*

tures, Blackwell, Oxford

Kovacs, M. L. and Cropley, A. J. (1975) *Immigrants and Society*, McGraw Hill, Sydney

Lambert, J. R. (1970) *Crime, Police and Race Relations*, London

Levi, R. (1957) *The Social Structure of Islam*, Cambridge University Press, Cambridge

Lindgren, H. C. (1969) *An Introduction to Social Psychology*, Wiley, New York

Listwan, I. A. (1960) 'Mental Disorders in Immigrants', *World Mental Health, 12*, 38—45

Little, A. (1975) 'The Educational Achievement of Ethnic Minority Children in London Schools' in G. K. Verma and C. Bagley (eds.), *Race and Education across Cultures*, Heinemann, London

Little, A. and Willey, R. (1981) *Multi-Ethnic Education: The Way Forward*, Schools Council, London (Schools Council Pamphlet No 18)

Little, A., Mabey, C. and Whitaker, G. (1968) 'The Education of Immigrant Pupils in Inner London Primary Schools', *Race, 9*, 439—452

Luria, A. R. (1961) *The Role of Speech in the Regulation of Normal and Abnormal Behaviour*, Pergamon, London

McDavid, J. W. and Harari, H. (1968) *Social Psychology*, Harper and Row, New York

McGlashan, G. (1972) 'Mugging — Who are the Victims?', *Race Today*, November, pp. 337—339

Miller, H. (1969) 'The Effectiveness of Teaching Technique for Reducing Colour Prejudice', *Liberal Education, 16*, 25—31

Milner, C. (1975) *Children and Race*, Penguin, Harmondsworth

Mohr, B. (1977) 'Ausländische Schüler in der Bundesrepublik Deutschland', *Bildung und Wissenschaft*, No 12, 185—211

Moses, R., Daniels, H. and Gundlach, R. (1977) 'Children's Language and the Multicultural Classroom' in D. E. Cross, G. C. Baker and L. J. Stiles (eds.), *Teaching in a Multicultural Society*, New York, Free Press

Mullard, C. (1973) *Black Britain*, George, Allen and Unwin, London

Newcomb, T. (1950) *Social Psychology*, Dryden, New York

Nicol, A. R. (1971) 'Psychiatric Disorder in the Children of Caribbean Immigrants', *Journal of Child Psychology and Psychiatry, 12*, 273—287

Nicol, A. R. (1974) 'The Problems faced by Young Immigrants', *The Practitioner, 213*, 329—334

NUT, (1981) *After the Fire: A Report on Education in St. Paul's, Bristol, and Multi-Ethnic Education in Avon*, Avon Division of National Union of Teachers, Bristol

OECD, (1974) *Creativity of the School*, OECD, Paris (Technical Report No 1)

Paulston, C. B. (1978) 'Education in a Bi/Multilingual Setting', *International Review of Education, 24*, 309—328

Peace, W. M. (1971) 'A Study of the Infant School Progress of a Group of Asian Immigrant Children', *English for Immigrants, 4,*

Philpott, S. B. (1977) 'The Montserratians: Migration Dependency and the Maintenance of Island ties in England, in J. L. Watson (ed.), *Between Two Cultures*, Blackwell, Oxford

Power, J. (1979) *Migrant Workers in Western Europe and the United States*, Pergamon, Oxford

Pratt, M. (1980) *Mugging as a Social Problem*, Routledge and Kegan Paul, London

Putniņš, A. L. (1976) 'Immigrant Adjustment: A Note on Kovacs' and Cropley's Model', *Australian Journal of Social Issues, 11*, 208—212

Rai, U. (1978) 'Between Cultures and Languages in "Little India"', *Times Educational Supplement*, 6th October, p. 11

Regan, J. O. and Cropley, A. J. (1964) 'Directional Set in Serial, Perceptual-Motor Tasks', *Perceptual and Motor Skills, 19*, 579—586

Richmond, A. H. (1967) *Post-War Immigrants in Canada*, University of Toronto Press, Toronto

Rist, R. (1978) *Guestworkers in Germany. The Chances for*

Pluralism, Praeger, New York

Rose, E. J. B. (with others) (1969) *Colour and Citizenship: A Report on British Race Relations*, Oxford University Press, London

Rutter, M., Yule, B., Morton, J. and Bagley, C. (1975) 'Children of West Indian Immigrants — III. Home Circumstances and Family Patterns', *Journal of Child Psychology and Psychiatry, 16*, 105—123

Rutter, M., Yule, W., Berger, M., Yule, B., Morton, J. and Bagley, C. (1974) 'Children of West Indian Immigrants — I. Rates of Behavioural Deviance and of Psychiatric Disorder', *Journal of Child Psychology and Psychiatry, 15*, 241—262

Sanua, V. D. (1970) 'Immigration, Migration and Mental Illness: A Review of the Literature with Special Emphasis on Schizophrenia' in E. B. Brody (ed.), *Behaviour in New Environments: Adaptation of Migrant Populations*, Sage, Beverly Hills

Saunders, M. (1980) 'The School Curriculum for Ethnic Minority Pupils: A Contribution to a Debate', *International Review of Education, 26*, 31—47

Schubert, J. and Cropley, A. J. (1972) 'Verbal Regulation of Behaviour and IQ in Canadian Indian and White Children', *Developmental Psychology, 7*, 295—301

Smolicz, J. J. and Secombe, M. J. (1977) 'A Study of Attitudes to the Introduction of Ethnic Languages and Cultures in Australian Schools', *Australian Journal of Education, 21*, 1—24

Steedman, H. (1979) 'The Education of Migrant Workers' Children in EEC Countries: From Assimilation to Cultural Pluralism', *Comparative Education, 15*, 259—268

Stenhouse, L. (1975) 'Problems of Research in Teaching about Race Relations' in G. K. Verma and C. Bagley (eds.), *Race and Education across Cultures*, Heinemann, London

Taft, R. (1953) 'The Shared Frame-of-Reference Concept applied to the Assimilation of Immigrants', *Human Relations, 6*, 45—46

Taft, R. (1966) *From Stranger to Citizen*, Tavistock, London

Taylor, F. (1974) *Race, School and Community*, NFER, Slough

Taylor, J. H. (1976) *The Half-Way Generation*, NFER, Slough

Thomas, W. I. and Znaniecki, F. (1958) *The Polish Peasant in Europe and America*, Knopf, New York

Titone, R. (1978) 'Psychological Aspects of Multilingual Education', *International Review of Education, 24,* 283—294

Townsend, H. E. R. and Brittan, E. M. (1972) *Organization in Multiracial Schools*, NFER, Slough

Townsend, H. E. R. and Brittan, E. M. *Multi-Racial Education: Need and Innovation*, Evans and Methuen, London

Triandis, H. C. and Lambert, W. W. (eds.) (1980) *Handbook of Cross-Cultural Psychology*, Allyn and Bacon, Boston

Tsiakalos, G. (1978) 'Situation und Probleme ausländischer Kinder und Jugendlicher in der Bundesrepublik', *Theorie und Praxis der Sozialpädagogik, 86,* 137—146

Tyehurst, L. (1951) 'Displacement and Migration', *American Journal of Psychiatry*, 107, 561—568

Verma, G. K. and Bagley, C. (1975) 'Curriculum Studies — Introduction' in G. K. Verma and C. Bagley (eds.), *Race and Education across Cultures*, Heinemann, London

Verma, G. K. and Bagley, C. (eds.) (1979) *Race, Education and Identity*, Macmillan, London

Verma, G. K. and Mallick, H. (1978) 'Social, Personal and Academic Problems of Ethnic Minority Pupils in British Schools', Paper presented at the International Congress of Applied Psychology, Munich, Federal Republic of Germany, July 30th—August 5th

Vygotsky, L. S. (1962) *Thought and Language*, Wiley, New York

Watson, J. L. (ed.) (1977) *Between Two Cultures*, Blackwell, Oxford

Weinberg, M. (1976) 'A Historical Framework for Multicultural Education' in D. E. Cross, G. C. Baker and L. J. Stiles (eds.), *Teaching in a Multicultural Society*, Free

Press, New York

Weinreich, P. (1979) 'Cross-Ethnic Identification and Self-Rejection in a Black Adolescent' in G. K. Verma and C. Bagley (eds.), *Race, Education and Identity*, Macmillan, London (a)

Weinreich, P. (1979) 'Ethnicity and Adolescent Identity Conflicts' in V. S. Kahn (ed.), *Minority Families in Britain*, Macmillan, London (b)

Wiles, S. (1968) 'Children from Overseas', *Institute of Public Relations Newsletter*, February, p. 84

Wood, M. (1934) *The Stranger: A Study in Social Relationships*, AMS Press, New York (1969 Reprint)

Zubrzycki, J. (1964) *Settlers of the Latrobe Valley: A Sociological Study of Immigrants in the Brown Coal Industry in Australia*, Australian National University Press, Canberra

Index

Abraham, A. S., 180
Adjustment
  ambivalence, 71
  detachment-attachment,
    13, 18, 100, 101
  jobs and, 99
  mutual, 40
  norms and, 61
  problems, 11
  rhetoric of the return,
    18, 19
  way of life, 62
Akpinar, U., 118
Alienation
  avoiding, 171
  crime and, 12, 103, 104, 117,
    122, 123
  culture shock and, 95
  delinquency and, 122
  dicrimination and, 106
  dual, 99—100, 104
  English language and, 135
  ghettoes and, 99
  groups and, 121
  internal, 95
  job, 94
  mother tongue and, 168
  school and, 138
  self-, 106, 121, 122, 138, 158
Anderson, C. C., 56
Assimilation
  approaches to, 135—136
  bicultural, 90
  dual, 101
  external, 89
  give-and-take in, 137
  internal, 89
  monistic, 91, 136, 171, 186
  multicultural, 92, 152
  mutual accomodation, 92
  partial, 104
  resistance to, 91
  school policy, 151—152
  shared frames of reference, 92
Åstedt, I., 179

Bagley, C., 28, 31, 32, 33, 34, 36,
    37, 82, 85, 102, 103, 106, 108,
    118, 119, 120, 132, 137, 138,
    143, 153, 154, 158, 164, 173,
    177
Ballard, C. and R., 87, 90, 101,
    107, 109, 111, 112, 113
Bart, M., 120
Bendit, R., 118
Berger, M., 37
Berry, J. W., 82
Bhatnagar, J. K., 33
Bilingualism, 123, 145, 160,
    161—162, 165
Black pride, 101
Black studies, 171, 172
Blomqvist, K., 179
Bloom, B. S., 47
Bogardus, E. S., 50
Brah, A., 115
Brittan, E. M., 32, 33, 120, 127,
    128, 130, 133, 140, 157, 172, 173
Brody, E. B., 99
Brown, L., 48
Bruner, J. S., 54

Calvet, L.-J., 162
Chain of culture, 113
Change
  adjusting to, 11
  in the homeland, 100
  in Pakistan, 64
  unawareness of, 114
Christopher, L., 33
Coard, B., 121
Coard, P., 121
Collard, D., 82
Commission for Racial
  Equality, 51, 52, 86, 180
Counselling, 183
Craft, M., 181
Creôle, 143, 167, 168, 179
Crime, 12, 103, 104, 117, 122, 123
Cropley, A. J., 18, 19, 22, 30, 31,
    43, 55, 56, 91, 99, 101, 102,
    106, 109, 112, 117, 145, 166,
    178, 185

Cross, D. E., 127, 169, 175, 176
Culture
    chain of, 113
    external aspects of, 40
    internal aspects of, 40
    language and, 56, 161
    norms and, 79
    portability of, 40
    shock, 95
    toleration of, 176
Cummins, J., 166
Curriculum
    adaptation of, 154
    change of perspective, 176
    elimination of stereotypes, 139
    failure to adjust, 130—131
    Green Paper of 1977, 134
    guidelines for, 14
    migrant culture in, 140
    multicultural, 169, 171 ff
    multi-ethnic, 134
    racism in, 87
    Schools Council projects, 144,
        154—155
    self-image and, 131

Dahya, B., 98
Dalbey, R. O., 89
Daniels, H., 141
Dargent, A., 154
David, H. P., 102
Delinquency
    among immigrant children, 30,
        36, 117
    self-alienation and, 122
Department of Education and
    Science, 34
Deslonde, J., 130, 132
Developmental estrangement, 111
Discrimination
    as alibi, 86
    ghettoes and, 99
    identity conflict and, 108
    job, 52, 85, 86, 94
    legal, 88
    mugging and, 103
    racial, 12, 40, 87
    residential, 85
Doston, G. A., 127, 169, 175
Double bind, 97, 103, 114, 124, 163
Dove, L., 114
Driver, G., 34, 120

Education
    achievement of migrants, 13
        actions taken, 13
        dispersal policy, 133
        double bind and, 114
        language and, 124
        mono-ethnic, 135
        multicultural, 134
        multi-ethnic, 134, 135
        multiracial, 14, 134
        psychological factors in, 13
        role of, 154
Egger, E., 54, 123
Eisenstadt, S. N., 103
Elizabeth I, 83
Emigration
    financing of, 70
    push-pull factors in, 20—21
    reasons for, 19—20
    role in society, 20
    traditions of, 21, 76
    world wars and, 70
England, R., 40
Estrangement, 13, 15, 18, 91, 100
Ethnic coexistence, 136
Ethnic reinforcement, 139
Ethnocentrism
    in lesson content, 175
    in text books, 177
Exaggerated ethnicity, 109, 116, 123

Fisher, S., 155
Fitzherbert, K., 75
Foner, N., 24, 74, 75, 76, 77, 78, 85
    100, 106, 111, 112

Gastarbeiter, 19, 26, 118
Garrison, L., 135, 138
Ghetto
    buffer mechanism, 99
    ethnic communities, 96, 98, 150
    factors promoting, 91, 99
    linking points, 99
    positive aspects, 98, 99
    school measures, 140
    voluntary formation, 68, 97
Glottophagie, 162
Goutman, R., 128
Groups
    admission to, 51
    alienation and, 121
    belongingness, 53
    consequences, 51
    definition, 50
    language and, 161

stereotyping and, 81
Gundlach, R., 141

Hammet, J., 102
Hansen, M. L., 111
Happel, M., 127, 169, 175
Harari, H., 43, 50
Harris, M., 111
Hicks, D. W., 155
Hiro, D., 72
Honey, J., 124, 142, 168
Hurrelmann, K., 129

Identity
    assimilation and, 101, 104
    conflict, 108, 158
    confusion, 104, 121—122
    crisis, 135
    cultural v. personal, 121
    development, 110
    homeland and, 63
    language and, 57, 58, 161
    problems, 110
    reclamation, 139
    school and, 138, 158
    society and, 42, 46
Immigrants
    age structure of, 31—32
    areas of concentration, 15, 32
    characteristics of, 20
    contamination of, 107
    contribution to life in Britain,
        92—93
    definition, 17—18, 26—27
    differences among, 27—29
    educational standards, 77
    estrangement among, 13, 15
    family size, 32
    homeownership among, 85
    mental health among, 99, 102,
        103, 104
    occupational status of, 15, 16,
        22, 28
    personal problems of, 11
    pioneers, 77
    politics and, 93
    recruiting, 20, 23
    rejection of, 12, 22, 28, 81
    school situation of, 28
    socio-economic status of, 11, 28
    unemployment among, 85, 94
    visibility, 89
Immigrant children

academic achievement of,
    33—35, 120
acceptance of British norms, 107
adaptation to receiving society,
    30, 105
adjustment problems, 105—106
attitudes for success, 140
conflict with parents, 112—113,
    141
definition of, 29—30, 105
delinquency among, 30, 36, 117
distribution in schools, 32
emotional disturbances, 118
family background, 119
fitting in in Britain, 139
half-second generation, 30, 105
identity conflict, 108, 158
language acquisition, 106, 141—2
misbehaviour of, 36
norms and, 61
reaction to rejection, 106, 109
role of homeland, 107
second generation, 30, 105
self-alienation, 122, 158
self-esteem, 107
social problems of, 36
socialization and, 30—31, 105
special care placement, 37
Immigrant newspapers, 183
Immigration
    chain, 77
    commencement of, 23
    historical development, 21—22
    internal, 64
    legislation on, 22—25
    policy, 14, 23, 24, 134
Innoculation effect, 157
Integration
    dual, 90
    education and, 13
    primary v. secondary, 89
    vocational, 90
Interest relations, 22

Jansen, C. J., 20
Jeffcoate, R., 34, 84, 87, 101, 107,
    108, 109, 118, 120, 121, 122,
    127, 128, 130, 131, 132, 133,
    137, 139, 143, 154, 158, 159,
    164, 170, 172, 173, 175, 176,
    177
Jeffrey, P., 18, 64, 96, 97
Jobs

discrimination, 52, 85—86, 87,
    94
group membership and, 52
influence of immigrants on
    market, 93
immigrants and, 15, 16
racism and, 87
recruiting practices, 20, 52
John, A., 113
Jones, C., 28, 85, 97
Jupp, J., 111

Kavass, I., 91
Keniston, K., 111
Khan, V. S., 18, 29, 31, 61, 64, 65,
    67, 68, 69, 90, 96, 99, 100, 101,
    107, 112, 113, 114, 119
Kindergarten
attitudes and, 182, 187
bridge to majority society, 181
mother tongue and, 165
socialization and, 47, 181—182
Kinship
homeland and, 107
in Pakistan, 68
in West Indies, 72
Kovacs, M. L., 18, 22, 43, 91, 99,
    101, 102, 106, 109, 112, 117

Lambert, J. R., 117
Language
alienation and, 124, 135, 168
crash programmes, 143, 160
dialect, 142
difficulties in acquiring English,
    123, 157
ego-dynamic function of, 57,
    160, 163
family models of, 160, 166
general language orientation,
    166, 167
identity and, 57, 134, 161
language trap, 124, 168
nonstandard English, 142
norms and, 58, 123
picking up English, 134, 157,
    159, 167
prerequisite for success in
    Britain, 123, 143
psychodynamics of, 54, 123,
    143, 160
relations with parents and, 123
remedial instruction, 160

resistance to learning, 57,
    161—162, 166
school achievement and, 119,
    124, 166
second stage English, 159
socialization and, 55—56
standard English, 141, 159, 166
standard vernacular, 142
thinking and, 54—55
Language centres, 144, 146, 159
Language clubs, 184
Levi, R., 69
Lindgren, H. C., 81
Listwan, I. A., 111
Little, A., 28, 31, 34, 134, 159, 188
Lopez-Blasco, A., 118
Luria, A. R., 47, 55

Mabey, C., 34
Mallick, H., 16, 26, 32, 106, 108,
    118, 121, 169
McCarran-Walter Act, 21, 77
McDavid, J. W., 43, 50
McGlashan, G., 117
Mental health
assimilation and, 104
double bind and, 103
immigrant, 99, 102
Migrant ideology, 77
Miller, H., 157
Milner, C., 122
Mohr, B., 149
Morton, J., 25, 37, 85, 119
Moses, R., 141
Mother tongue
kindergarten and, 183, 188
language clubs and, 184
language of instruction, 145,
    148—150, 165
learning English and, 165, 168
linguistic base, 165
loss of, 145—146, 160, 163
multicultural schooling and, 169
threshold of competence and,
    166, 167
Mullard, C., 22, 23, 107, 121
Multiculturalism
lesson content and, 171 ff
multicultural approach, 92, 151
multicultural centres, 185
multicultural education, 128,
    169 ff
multicultural perspective, 175 ff
multicultural schooling, 169

multiracial education, 134

Newcomb, T., 50
Nicol, A. R., 36, 85, 102, 158
Norms
    adjustment and, 61—62
    assimilation and, 89—90, 101
    attitudinal paradox and, 84
    conflict between, 13, 80, 40, 41,
        58, 90, 96, 111—112, 115,
        140, 182
    culture and, 79, 95
    definition, 79—80
    differences between groups, 79
    dimensions of, 48
    dual alienation and, 100
    groups and, 28, 50
    homeland, 78
    internal v. external, 89—90
    kindergarten and, 182
    language and, 58
    learning of, 47—48
    media and, 79
    mental health and, 102
    schools and, 138
    society and, 44—46, 57, 79
NUT, 131, 135

OECD, 128
Oxfam image, 109, 176

Paulston, C. B., 106, 160, 161, 164,
    165, 166
Peace, W. M., 33
Personality, 39, 43, 49, 54, 101
Philpott, S. B., 29, 72, 74, 75, 76,
    78, 96
Piaget, J., 54
Police
    clashes with, 104
    hostility to, 107
    immigrants in, 93
Policy
    assimilation, 150
    British Nationality Act, 24
    citizenship, 24, 53
    concentration, 151
    dispersal, 133, 150
    Green Paper of 1977, 134
    immigration, 14, 23
    need for, 186
    West German, 147, 150
    White Paper of 1983, 180

Power, J., 84, 85, 87, 102
Pratt, M., 103, 117
Prejudice
    against immigrants, 12, 40, 84
    against majority society, 83, 183
    alibi, 86
    approaches in school, 153—154
    attitudinal paradox and, 84
    crime and, 104
    definition, 82—83
    denial of, 84
    ghettoes and, 99
    history of, 83
    in children, 158
    racial, 53, 84, 98, 119—120
    reverse, 101
Psychological tests, 177—178
Putniņš, A. L., 90, 101

Racial climate, 159
Racial self-respect, 138, 149
Racism
    children and, 108—109, 158, 170
    combating in school, 154,
        158—159
    curriculum and, 131
    institutional v. individual, 87
    official, 87—88
    schools and, 87, 139, 177
Regan, J. O., 55
Rejection
    of Britain by immigrants,
        95—97, 100, 183
    ghettoes, 99
    self-, 59, 121
Remedial instruction, 144, 150
Remittances, 64
Remittance economy, 21
Rhetoric of the return, 18, 19
Richmond, A. H., 18
Rist, R., 149, 151
Rose, E. J. B., 19
Rutter, M., 28, 37, 85, 119

Sanua, V. D., 102
Saunders, M., 92, 97, 130, 131, 154
School
    achievement of immigrants, 13,
        33—36, 120
    assimilation policy in, 151
    attitude change in, 153
    attitudes of immigrant
        children to, 107

conflict of norms in, 78, 114
conservative v. transforming
  role, 128
double bind and, 114
ESN classes, 143
identity problems and, 138, 158
immigrant parents and, 183—184
integration and, 13
inter- v. intrapersonal role, 129
language and, 124, 141
mediator of norms, 127—128
racism in, 87
self-image and, 129, 130, 137
socialization in, 127, 138
Schools Council, 14, 134, 144, 154
Schubert, J., 56, 178
Secombe, M. J., 90, 101, 136
Self-
  alienation, 158
  contempt, 121
  doubt, 158
  esteem, 120, 171
Self-image
  achievement and, 120
  English language and, 163, 164
  national, 42
  school and, 129, 131
  strengthening, 137, 139
  unfavourable, 119
Selznick, P., 48
Semilingualism, 145—146, 160, 165
Sentiment relations, 22
Sex roles, 69, 74, 113
Smolicz, J. J., 90, 101, 136
Social accommodation, 154
Socialization
  conflict in, 111
  conformity and, 47
  groups and, 50
  homeland and, 63
  immigrant children and, 30—31
  language and, 55—56, 58
  primary, 31, 47
  secondary, 31, 47
Socio-economic status
  immigrants', 97, 118
  language learning and, 160, 165,
    167
  in West Indies, 74
Special classes, 144—145, 148,
  150—151, 159
Steedman, H., 30, 33, 61, 95, 118,
  142, 146, 152, 160, 169, 175

Stenhouse, L., 153, 154, 159
Stereotypes
  children's, 82, 108—109
  national self-, 41, 43
  of immigrants, 62, 81—82
  Oxfam image, 109, 176
  school role in eliminating, 139
  Tarzan image, 109, 176
Stiles, L. J., 127, 169, 175
Stop rules, 56
SUS-Law, 88

Taft, R., 89, 91, 92
Taylor, F., 143, 144, 159
Taylor, J. H., 19, 21, 28, 33, 34, 64,
  67, 70, 82, 85, 86, 94, 98, 112,
  113, 114, 117
Teachers
  mother tongue, 145, 148, 179
  peripatetic, 145
  prejudice and, 132
  relationship with pupils, 159
  role of, 177
  special qualifications, 180
Teacher training, 180—181
Thomas, W. I., 30
Titone, R., 57, 123, 160
Townsend, H. E. R., 16, 27, 32, 33,
  120, 127, 128, 130, 133, 140,
  143, 157, 159, 172, 173, 188,
  189
Triandis, H. C., 48
Tsiakalos, G., 187
Tutoring, 185
Tyehurst, L., 102

Verma, G. K., 16, 26, 31, 32, 82,
  107, 108, 118, 119, 121, 137,
  138, 153, 154, 158, 169, 173
Visibility, 89
Vygotsky, L. S., 54

Watson, J. L., 17, 21
Weinberg, M., 131, 136, 170
Weinreich, P., 121
Wiles, S., 23, 34
Willey, R., 134, 135, 188
Wong, S., 120
Wood, M., 22

Yule, B., 28, 37, 85, 119
Zia ul-Haq, 66
Zimmer, J., 118
Znaniecki, F., 30
Zubrzycki, J., 111